MW00636931

The Deacon
and
The Doctor

A Prescription for
Navigating Child Loss

Deacon Gerard-Marie Anthony
and
Dr. Sabine Heisman

En Route Books and Media, LLC
Saint Louis, Missouri

En Route Books and Media, LLC
5705 Rhodes Avenue
St. Louis, MO 63109

Hand Drawn Illustration by:
Rikhil and Rheiya Thuramalla

Copyright © 2022 TXu002299409
Gerard-Marie Anthony and Sabine Heisman

ISBN-13: 978-1-956715-39-2
Library of Congress Control Number 2022935678

Scripture quotations in this work are taken from two translations of the Bible: *The New American Bible, revised edition and New Revised Standard Version Bible: Catholic Edition.*

Scripture texts in this work are taken from the *New American Bible, revised edition* © 2010, 1991, 1986, 1970 Confraternity of Christian Doctrine, Washington, D.C. and are used by permission of the copyright owner. All Rights Reserved. No part of the New American Bible may be reproduced in any form without permission in writing from the copyright owner.

Scripture Verses are taken from the *New Revised Standard Version Bible*: Catholic Edition, copyright 1989, 1993, Division of Christian Education of the National Council of the Churches of Christ in the United States of America. Used by permission. All rights reserved.

All rights reserved. No part of this book may be reproduced or transmitted in any form, except for brief quotations, without written permission from the authors or publisher.

To Mary, Mother of Life

To all mothers who have ever lost a child. May this book help you to have peace and know that your loved one is in our prayers.

A Mom's Peace. May you continue to be an instrument of God's love to all who have entrusted their little ones to God's loving arms.

To All the Children who are now embraced by the Merciful Arms of our Heavenly Father…Jesus, I trust in you.

Table of Contents

Appendices

In Memoriam

Francis Palladino

Brenden Gerard Lee Meier

Regina Palladino

Innocent Bobick

Stella Palladino

Micah and Asher French

Thomas Palladino

Monica Mary Pearl

William Matthew Balint

Liguori Mary Pearl

Karen Elaine Balint

Julian Mary Pearl

Gabriel Sullivan

Isaiah Roodhouse

Lucy Sullivan

Siena and Francisco
  Heisman

Dominic Sullivan

Celeste Allen

Mary Sullivan

Raymond Sullivan

Gabrielle Lythea Anthony

Baby Girl Anthony

Xavier Francis Rodriguez

Erick Javier Gonzalez
  Chavarria

Anne Marie Blaicher

Ambrose Chiara Blaicher

Andrew Joseph McLaughlin

Jonathan O' Tormey

Katharine Louise Reintjes

Frances Cabrini Reintjes

Emeht Alan Wood

Royce Hasim Thomas

Mark William Erwin

Lucy Rose Erwin

Clare Meredith Pomilla

Zelie Maria Pomilla

Micah French

Asher French

Charlie Hamilton

Thomas Aquinas Gossin

Baby Boy Marconyak

Stephen Marconyak

Cooper Cobos

Gianna Cobos

Thomas Cobos

Riley Cobos

Reagan Cobos

Ruth Ann Krall

Joseph Luke Krall

Mary Murphy

Michael Gabriel

Kelly Scheetz

Emmett & Brigid Wilmes   Aidan Michael Muni

Rose Vasquez   Simon Maristella Cautero

Hope Vasquez   Little P & R Towey

Iggy Vasquez   Alexander Ambrose Huff

G.W.A. Vasquez   Tobias Bonilla

Lily M. Vasquez   Bianca Bonilla

Christopher C. Vasquez   Clara Bonilla

Seton Elizabeth Cautero   Sebastian James Towey

....and all the babies served by A Mom's Peace

Introductions

"The Doctor"

In 2016, I heard five words no parent wants to hear, "I can't find a heartbeat." In that moment, the existence I had so carefully cultivated was instantly shattered. Nothing would ever be the same after the loss of my twins. In the immediate aftermath, I could not catch my breath. I struggled to breathe for weeks after the loss. I was certain that there was a physical cause, that somehow the two D&C (Dilation & Curettage) procedures I endured to remove the twins had caused a pulmonary embolism. I sought a medical solution to what I assumed was a medical issue. At the burials (we had two as the twins were removed a week apart), I was so short of breath and could barely stand upright. Even with all the emotional trauma all I could focus on was "why can't I breathe?" As a clinical psychologist, I would have told a patient that trauma can result in physical symptoms, but as a mother, all I could do was struggle for air. I knew that one in four pregnancies ended in loss. I knew it in my mind, I knew it as a professional, but as a mother to a healthy, beautiful, living boy, I did not accept it as a reality for my life. I was wrong.

We knew we wanted to bury our babies but there were very limited options to bury children lost through miscarriage. My husband tried desperately to call our parish priests, the archdiocese, and funeral homes, with no luck. No one seemed to know what to do with a loss before 28 weeks. Somehow, we were given the name of Kara Palladino, founder of the nonprofit organization, A Mom's Peace. Kara Palladino founded A Mom's Peace to help families with the aftermath of miscarriages and stillbirths, specifically helping with burying their babies. She lost several children through miscarriage and struggled to find a place to bury her first loss. So, feeling called by God, she decided to start A Mom's Peace, and thanks to the wonderful Benedictine Sisters of Virginia, a dedicated space (St. Andrew's) was created to bury miscarried and still born children.

There was a small sense of peace knowing a place existed where I could visit and mourn my precious children. I also met Deacon Gerard-Marie Anthony through the organization, and we tried to help other mothers/families as best we could, spiritually and psychologically. We had many discussions: his perspective, a spiritual one, and mine, a medical/psychological model. Most times we agreed, sometimes we did not, but ultimately, we realized that together we could collaborate on something that might help others attempting to survive tragedy. You'll notice the Deacon and I often use different terminology and may not always agree on our prescriptions, but our goal is to present different perspectives and different interventions to help mothers and families who have experienced child loss on their journey of trans-for-mation and acceptance. This book is very much a dialogue between science and faith, and yes, they can coexist. Our voices and contributions are different and sometimes at odds, but we approached this project with respect for each other's beliefs and professional contributions. We labeled the sections for clarity so you can see the sections written from psychological and clerical perspectives.

Ultimately, the hope for this book is to provide a pre-scriptive dialogue that may help you navigate the ever-evolving grief one experiences after losing a child. Please note, I will not use the term healing or recovery because I am not quite certain one ever truly heals or recovers from child loss, but you can survive and learn to thrive again. The grief does change, it does soften, and you will survive, you will be transformed, and you will breathe again!

"The Deacon"

There is a beautiful quote that I think summarizes the journey of losing a child. The quote is one we placed in our A Mom's Peace virtual Garden of Remembrance, which says, "Some people say you are too painful to remember. I say you are too precious to forget." Every single child that is lost through miscarriage or stillbirth can be a painful memory, but also a precious life that is never to be forgotten. We write this book to help you understand that pain and joy are part of the grief journey to find peace; and embracing both is how we come to a place of acceptance. Scientifically speaking, when all of the body works in harmony, we call it homeostasis; from a spiritual perspective, we seek peace. Peace is when there is harmony among all parts of life united in love.

An important part of life is grieving. Often, people ask how long will you mourn your child? The answer is just as love does not die, neither does the grieving process. You will love your children until your last breath. Love does not exist only in times of joy but engulfs tough times in an ocean of love, so it is transformed. Just as medicine does not ignore a disease, but instead focuses on it to treat it, we must transform our conceptualization of losing a child through miscarriage or stillbirth. This book seeks to find an effective prescription to help families reach a place of acceptance to achieve a new homeostasis through transformation so they can thrive as God intended; to be in a place where you do not just get by in life, but live life to the fullest as God intends (see Jn. 10:10).

This transformation is especially important in situations of miscarriage and stillbirth, in which we often think "I'll be happy when." We try to convince ourselves that life will be better after we can just "go back to the way things were before", or we are told things will get better when we "have another baby." Then we get frustrated that the kids aren't "old enough" and we think we'll be more content when they are older. Or, we're frustrated that we have teenagers to deal with! We tell ourselves that our life will be complete when our spouse gets his or her act together, when we get a nicer car, when we are able to go on a nice vacation or when we retire. We keep making up reasons to wait for life to get better!

The truth is there's no better time to work towards being happy than right now. If not now, when? Your life will always be filled with challenges, but you <u>can</u> rest in the Lord. So, treasure every moment you have and treasure it more because you shared it with someone special, that little one who is now entrusted to the mercy of God. Happiness may look different now to those who have experienced child loss, but we can go forward in peace. As St. John of the Cross notes, **"Happiness is not a destination, it's a method of travel" or a journey.** We propose the way from pain to peace involves a seven-fold journey of the soul and mind. As the Psalm says, "Seven times a day I praise you, because your judgments are righteous. Lovers of your law have much peace; for them there is no stumbling block" (Ps. 119: 164-165). Each part of the journey is a precious pearl. Bishop Joseph Perry reminds us:

> You see a pearl comes from an oyster which is soft, but stays tightly closed to protect itself. The only time it opens up is when it takes in water to breathe. Sometimes when it takes in water however, a microscopic pebble, a

piece of sand, may enter. This is painful for the oyster, but it keeps the pebble within. Over time it forms a lining over the sand and then another lining, then another one, and the result is something beautiful because that is how a pearl is made.

It is the same with each of these aspects of healing. They may feel like a painful pebble or like we're breathing in sand, but when united to the heart of God, it can be transformed into a hymn of praise or a beautiful pearl since love can bring "much peace."

So, let us take this journey together learning lessons from life, love, and taking time to A.C.Q.U.I.R.E peace:

A = Attain Knowledge and Prudence (What to Say and Not to Say)

C= Care for the Mind (Psychology)

Q= Questions about the Body's Response to Miscarriage/Still birth (Medical)

U= Unlocking God's Perspective (Spiritual Aspects)

I= Intersecting Family Perspectives (Family Responses to Grief)

R= Relationships with Others (Society and Friends/Community Support)

E= Engagement in Healing

We as the Deacon and the Doctor hope to be good guides with powerful prescriptions along with Scripture, God's healing word, which is meant to "equip us with every good work" (2Tim. 3:17), especially the work that helps you *ACQUIRE* peace, homeostasis, and Spiritual nourishment for your journey.

Prescription 1

Attain Knowledge and Prudence
Community Response/Guidance

What to Do and Not to Do

"Let no evil talk come out of your mouths, but only what is useful for building up, as there is need, so that your words may give grace to those who hear"-Ephesians. 4:29

Community Response: What to do and What not to do!

Child loss is not often discussed in society. This is unfortunate because so many women and families go through this experience, often alone. We hope to help our readers navigate both the painful journey of loss and grief, but also, how to respond to misguided well-wishers and society in general during an already difficult time.

From personal experience, let me (the Doctor) share, there are indeed right and wrong things to say to a woman who has suffered a miscarriage or stillbirth. In fact, we are going to give you a list because despite people's best intentions, sometimes people lack common sense when it comes to addressing death. They, in fact, may do things that make grieving harder and make things down-right awkward at best and more painful at worst. Mothers are often in shock after their loss and sometimes do not know how to respond to others' attempts to comfort them, especially when what they are saying makes things worse. Initially you are so over-whelmed that you do not know how to respond. We also often feel guilty for expressing our feelings to people who are trying to help, but we must self-advocate. Since people often do not know how to respond appropriately, we can educate them. It is not easy, but it is necessary. It is so important to let people know what we do and do not need/or want while grieving. Below are some statements you may hear after your loss and some advice on how to respond.

FYI, I heard all of these after the loss of my twins.

Things NOT to say (Doctor's Perspective)

"At least you know you can get pregnant!"

(This was said by my doctor 90 seconds after the sono-gram revealed my babies had died).

This is not what anyone needs to hear after the loss of a child. It does not change the fact that they just lost their child. People assume it is comforting, but it invalidates the experience of the loss of the child that just passed. If you are able to successfully get pregnant and have another child, it certainly <u>does not</u> replace the one that died. This implicitly degrades the child of his or her unique dignity because the child becomes some*thing* to replace instead of some*one* who is loved. Also, five years later, I have never been able to get pregnant again.

Suggested Response: I appreciate you are trying to help me be hopeful; but there's no positive way to spin this. Even if I successfully get pregnant again and have another child, it will never be able to replace the baby I just lost or the lifetime I was supposed to share with <u>this</u> baby.

Implication: Here's why this is not an appropriate thing to say to a grieving family. First, the mother may or may not actually be able to get pregnant again. Second, another pregnancy will never, ever, ever, replace the baby that died. Third, it completely makes the child who just died seem insignificant in the grand scheme of things. Life does not continue the same way for people who lost a baby because they did not just lose a baby, they lost countless birthdays, holidays, graduations, special moments. <u>They lost an entire lifetime!</u> Every time there is a holiday or a beginning of the school year picture, they will think to themselves, what would their baby look like now, at age 3, age 5, age 15, age 25. Every time they see a child around the age their child WOULD HAVE been, they feel the loss. There are constant, lifelong reminders everywhere that their child, that beautiful irreplaceable child, is gone.

"At least it was early."

How does that make it any easier? Whether it was five weeks, ten weeks, twenty-five weeks, or +40 weeks, the grief you experience after losing a child you carried inside of you does not depend on how long you carried the baby. I think people who have not felt the pain of child loss believe because you carried a child for a short time, somehow that means you did not have the chance to bond with the baby or dream about the child's future. What they do not understand is that you did not just lose a child after X number of weeks. YOU LOST AN ENTIRE LIFE! You lost a lifetime of birthdays, holidays, milestones. When you are pregnant you start imagining the life of that child and all the beautiful things to come.

Suggested Response: I loved that baby every minute it was inside me, and I will love the baby every minute I am alive because that's what a mother does.

Implication: It is important for people to understand, how long you loved and carried a child does not correlate with how long you grieve, because you did not just lose a few weeks or months, you lost a lifetime. I have spoken with mothers who have lost children to miscarriage who still mourn decades after their loss. They have continued to live their lives and have happiness, but they never forgot the baby they lost. Losing a child at <20 weeks does not make the death of the child any easier. I can personally guarantee you that! To imply that the grief is any less severe or significant because of the timing of the loss is hurtful to the grieving mother/family.

**"Well, I mean it wasn't really a baby, right?
I mean it wasn't actually born."**

No, just no! Regardless of your political or religious beliefs, this is not an okay statement. The mother is clearly mourning! The person who said this certainly was not trying to be offensive, the implication was that since the baby hadn't been born the loss was somehow less significant.

Deacon Anthony also shares a story about statements like this:

> When I share with people, especially young adults, I am a part of an apostolate that works with families of miscarried babies in the wake of loss, they sometimes ask "Why do you bury a fetus? It is not a person, only a fetus so does it really matter?" Their child DOES matter to that family, regardless of how you feel about the topic of when life begins. Since it matters to the family; you have to

know if you're going to speak, you have to speak and act like it matters to you!"

Suggested Response: Please keep your political or "religious" beliefs to yourself. This baby was alive and real to us regardless of how long it lived. Even if you cannot understand the experience, either grieve with us compassionately or say nothing.

Implication: People have very passionate views on when life begins and when it ends. This is not a time to have a political or religious discussion. This is a time to either keep quiet or be compassionate. The mother/family are clearly grieving the loss of <u>their</u> child, so be respectful at the very least. If you disagree with the magnitude of their grief, then just keep quiet. If you cannot understand or relate, then just say, "I'm sorry for your loss," and leave them alone to grieve how they see fit.

"Everything happens for a reason."

This is an attempt to explain something that is unexplainable. It does not help! When you are grieving the loss of a child, all you know is the baby you expected to hold is gone. Some people get to know why their child passed (sometimes it was due to a medical issue, a genetic issue, a trauma, etc.), and for some it may help slightly soothe the pain, but for most women, we never know why the child died. The "everything happens for a reason" statement is made widely after the death of a loved one and people need to understand it is not comforting to be reminded you have little control over anything in your life. It often provokes more anxiety. One mother I worked with noted, "people keep saying that my baby died for a reason like it was some kind of favor, it's awful, it made me feel worse."

Suggested Response: I appreciate the thought, but while I may not know why my baby died, I know my baby died. That is the only fact that I know. The reason doesn't matter. I'm grieving and I know you are trying to help, but I just want my child back. Knowing or believing there is a reason that my child died is not comforting, in fact, it makes me more anxious to think I have so little control over my life.

Implication: Some people may say that if you know your child died due to some terrible genetic anomaly or would have had a difficult life due to a medical condition, that this was the reason the child passed, i.e., to spare them and you a lifetime of difficulty and pain. Still not comforting! With or without a reason, the death of a child is the death of a child. It is not comforting, but rather, incredibly anxiety provoking when people say to trust that "everything happens for a reason" because often you will never know the reason. Instead, say "We don't know why this happened, but I am so sorry for your loss. I am here if you need anything."

"God needed another angel."

This is the one that is most difficult for me to respond to because the person is clearly trying to be kind. It got to a point where if one more person said this, I felt like I was going to throw a chair! I understand their intent, but I eventually got so annoyed that I remember saying to a family member, "That makes no sense. God did not need another angel. There are plenty. My children are not angels, they are gone and that's all I can process right now." I'm not saying that was the right response, but when you lose a child, you have to give yourself a little bit of grace to self-advocate and protect yourself.

Suggested Response: (This may seem a little cheeky but… I just started saying), "I appreciate the thought, but babies don't become angels when they die. I would appreciate a prayer for my family." Perhaps that was because I was just annoyed. There is no right or wrong response to this.

If you are religious, you can say, instead," I appreciate you are trying to make me feel better but please just say a prayer for me and my family." If you are not religious or have different beliefs about death, then simply say, "That doesn't really follow my belief system, but I would appreciate your good thoughts or simply just grieve with me."

Implications: While well intentioned, the idea that God took my child specifically to become an angel or that the child became an angel is not founded in Catholic doctrine and frankly, doesn't make sense. I believe my children are in Heaven, and I will, hopefully, be reunited with them one day, but it is in no way comforting to think God specifically intervened to take my child away for his needs. Also, you may not know the specific religious beliefs of the family. If you do, you can offer a prayer, if not, then share you will be thinking of them and sending supportive thoughts in their time of grief.

As a side note, I would also make sure to be careful who you go to for religious counsel. I sought counsel from a local parish priest that I did not know well after my miscarriage because I actually had no idea what the Catholic Church taught about what happens to babies lost this way. In my case it was a horrible experience as the priest spent 45 minutes talking about how there's no way to know where the child is and to hope they were not lost forever and to just have faith. He dove deeply into doctrinal theory and basically lectured about not having an answer but to just have faith. It triggered a massive panic attack! On the recommendation of a friend, I went to see her priest at her parish and it was a completely different experience. The priest was kind, compassionate, and explained things like Baptism of Desire (which Deacon Anthony explains later in the book as well). He listened, he grieved with me, and he offered tangible hope that I would be reunited with my children. Perhaps ask a friend about referrals if you have religiously based questions. In my case, going the therapeutic route with a psychologist was more beneficial. I encourage you to make sure you are comfortable with whichever route you take. Also, you can always do both, or neither, sometimes support from friends and family is enough. In essence, seek help when you need it and from sources you trust but do not hesitate to seek a second or third or fourth opinion and then make your own informed decision.

"Are you still upset about this? Shouldn't you be over this by now, it was just a miscarriage?" (Actual statement made by a <u>friend</u>)

While initially angry at my friend for such a thoughtless comment, I realized unless you have lost a child, there is no way to understand the magnitude of the impact of the death of a child. And that is something I hoped they would never experience. The physical recovery of a miscarriage may be quick, but the emotional and psychological toll may be long-lasting.

Suggested Response: "I carried that child for every second of its life and I will love them for every second of mine. I will take as long as I need to, to process and accept this experience." As psychiatrist Dr. Parkes notes in his book, <u>Bereavement: Studies of Grief in Adult Life</u>, "The pain of grief is just as much part of life as the joy of love; it is perhaps the price we pay for love, the cost of commitment. To ignore this fact, or to pretend that it is not so, is to put on emotional blinkers which leaves us unprepared for the losses that will inevitably occur in our own lives and unprepared to help others cope with losses in theirs." A deceased son or daughter is not something to "get over," but a relationship, an experience, that will always be cherished.

<u>Implications:</u> Statements like the above imply there is a timeline for grieving. That is not the case. You perpetually feel the absence of the child you lost. People who have suffered child loss often describe that time feels/passes differently after the loss, as if you have one foot on earth and one foot in a different reality. The grief of losing a child DOES NOT END, it changes, it softens, but it does not end. Not a day has passed since my twins died that I don't think of them.

"Be grateful for the children you do have."
In my opinion, for this one, please be as cheeky in your response as you like! My personal response went something

like this, "You have 10 seconds to leave my presence before you and I have a problem."

Suggested Response: Mourning the child we lost does not in any way mean we are not grateful for the children we have. But, imagine if one of your children died, having others that survive would not in any way make the loss of one any less painful. Grieving does not mean we are ungrateful for the many blessings in our life.

Implications: This one absolutely infuriates me! The idea that grieving the loss of a child somehow makes you ungrateful makes no sense. Why can you not mourn the loss of one child while still being grateful for any living children that exist? Why are they mutually exclusive? The implication is the person is saying, stop feeling sad because you have other kids. It is both offensive and unhelpful.

****

Things NOT to say (Deacon's Perspective)

As a deacon, I also have some dos and don'ts for people trying to support mothers who have just experienced a miscarriage.

"We don't know where your baby is!"

Response: Sadly, this has been said to numerous mothers
(including the one who is co-writing this book as well as the
deacon's sister) when they ask if their child is with God.
Sometimes clergy panic and forget to be empathetic along
with upholding the dignity of the faith. As clergy, we have to
remember not to try and make the time right after the loss of
a child into a dogmatic presentation of the Faith WITHOUT
EMPATHY. Of course, we must always be rooted in truth as
there is no authentic charity without truth (see Eph. 4:15) but
notice the truth must be spoken in charity. At the time of
losing a child, it may not be the most charitable thing to
spend an hour debating what Scripture and the Catechism
say about the eternal destiny of that deceased baby. Keep it
warm and simple with something like, "The baby is now in
the loving embrace of our merciful Father." Then after some
time has passed, you can discuss the theology of what that
means if the family has more questions.

"Can you tell the mother to wait?"

Response: Yes, from a practical perspective people understand that Churches get busy and have schedules, but it is
crucial for churches and clergy to know there is an urgency
in doing funerals for miscarried babies. It should not be an
"afterthought" or "I'll do it when I get around to it."

Sometimes, I've seen clergy slip into an unintentional, but still hurtful mentality of "it's just a miscarriage." Child loss through miscarriage is just as traumatic as non-miscarriage child loss. The family may need a burial to help with closure. As clergy who are ordained to serve the people of God, we must put this as a higher priority on our schedules as no family should ever have to bury their child alone without the presence of the Church, nor should they have to wait until it is convenient for us as clergy to do so.

On that same note, however parents must sometimes realize that clergy may not have an opening to do the funeral until a few days after the miscarriage/stillbirth. Sometimes, I as a deacon, may have five funerals in a week as well as other pastoral work. So please know that sometimes it is not that your baby is unimportant, but the fact that there are only so many hours in a day.

Things NOT to do (Deacon's Perspective)

Do NOT keep this taboo!!!

There are families in various parishes where I work who have been holding back discussing their miscarriage for over 50 years...50 years!!!! This is something that needs to be talked about as there is an entire sisterhood of mothers out there who can help one another if the topic was just discussed instead of swept under the carpet.

As Dr. Heisman noted, "In all my years attending mass, I've never once heard miscarriage acknowledged or discussed in homilies or even mentioned in parish bulletins with referrals to help grieving families with this particular type of loss. One in four pregnancies ends in loss so clearly at least 25% of our community has been impacted by child loss either directly or indirectly. I don't understand why it is not discussed more at church."

Do NOT try to convince the mom or family to pretend like nothing happened.

Grace comes from living in reality! I've seen so many awkward conversations in which the mom or family is trying to find a shoulder to lean on and the community just wants to talk about football or the weather because it is an uncomfortable subject for them. That leads to the next item on this list.

Do NOT make it about you.

It is the family that is grieving so if the mom or family needs space, give them space. If they need someone to talk to, allow them to talk. Even if they need someone to cry with in order to process their grief, that's okay. Don't try to force things because that is what is convenient for you. Remember as St. Paul said, "Love is patient...it is not selfish" (1 Cor. 13:4-5).

Do NOT forget the mom and family are human beings, thus they have emotions and are not simply an abstract case study meant to follow a timeline.

People heal at different paces and the path to peace goes through different phases for different people. Do not think just because it has been six months since the mom has lost her child, she "should be over it" by now. Honestly, you do not "get over" losing a child. It's a traumatic event. You can however be resilient and become the best person you can be which includes adapting to the tough times in life.

So, we've covered what not to do, but what about how to help? Here are some things you can do that are helpful:

Things to say (Doctor's Perspective)

Acknowledge the Loss:

I cannot stress this enough, but even acknowledging the loss is incredibly helpful. Everyone is so uncomfortable with child loss they want to move past it as quickly as possible. For the first few weeks everyone asks, "How are you doing?" but what about six weeks later, six months later, on the anniversary of their death, holidays? Just because time passes, doesn't mean they forget. ACKNOWLEDGE THE LOSS, not just initially, but on milestones or holidays. Every Christmas, every "would have been" birthday, or milestone is painful. To know you are not alone in your grief, that someone remembers your child, is comforting. While we as a society do not seem comfortable discussing child loss, the parents of the child never forget. More importantly they <u>do not want</u> to forget their child. Trust me when I say it hurts more for people to pretend your beautiful child never existed. It implies the child did not matter enough to be remembered. Say their name! Remember them on important days and what would have been milestones. Believe me, the parents certainly don't forget!

Things TO SAY

1. I'm sorry for your loss. I am here for you however you need me to be.
2. You are not alone.
3. Be kind to yourself.
4. I'm thinking of you.
5. You are strong. You will survive. You will be different, but you will survive.
6. There is no timeline for grief. Take all the time you need and if you want to talk, please let me know.
7. Do you need company while you grieve?

8. I want to support you but I'm not sure how, so
    please let me know how I can help!
9. I want to give you space to grieve, but please know I
    am here for you anytime.
10. Can I bring over dinner for you and your family or
    take care of your other children so you can take
    some time to yourself?

DO:

Speak About the Loss:

Offer to talk about the baby. It is important to process
the experience. While it may be uncomfortable for both the
parents and the listener, it is critical to be able to speak <u>out
loud</u> about the loss. Sometimes it feels like people forgot your
child existed. Even if the loss was early, you continue to
mourn the baby. You as a parent don't forget, but it feels as
though everyone else did after a few months. People often
say they do not want to "remind" you of the loss. Several people said that to me when I asked why no one ever mentions
the twins. I often heard, "We didn't want to remind you." I
guarantee you, a mother who has suffered child loss does not
ever forget her child. Not a day goes by when I don't think of
my children constantly. As mothers, we think of our kids all
day! Did they eat enough? Are they safe? etc. What makes
you think we wouldn't also think of the children we lost? I

personally think I will see my kids again, so I often wonder, are they okay? Do they know how much I love them? Speak to the mother about <u>all</u> their children or ask if she wants to talk about it. The family may also need time before they are ready to speak and process the loss. Give them time but remember to ask every now and then if they would like to talk about their experience.

DO:

Honor the Baby:

One of the most meaningful things for me was being able to bury my babies and have a marker with their names at the cemetery. It was a tangible way to honor their existence. Their names forever carved in the beautiful stone was a way they would not be forgotten by the world. After a loss it seems the world wants to move on but you <u>never</u> "move on" from child loss. A beautiful thing to do for someone who has lost a baby is to honor them. Whether it is through providing a small, personalized object to commemorate the existence of the baby or a donation to a favorite charity in their honor, or even just remembering to say their name. SAY THEIR NAME! There is nothing more precious to me than when someone says my children's names. While they may not initially be able to tolerate having a keepsake honoring their children, a donation in the baby's name or the family's name is a beautiful way to acknowledge and honor the loss. Saying their names is a very simple yet meaningful way to honor them and helps the mother/family feel supported in their grief.

We are often asked by grieving families if they should name their baby. That is a very personal decision but I encourage you to do so. You do not have to do it right away if it's too emotionally triggering, but at some point, I urge you to consider naming your baby. Parents, especially those who have suffered an early pregnancy loss and do not know the gender of the baby, wonder the best way to name their children. As with most of the experience of a miscarriage, there are no set rules. There is the option to give the baby a gender-neutral name, the name of a favorite saint, or a name special to the family history. The objective is to honor the beautiful existence of the baby by acknowledging them with all the respect they are due.

DO:

Help the Family:

This one is a bit tricky. Initially, the family may want to be alone to grieve. Once it is appropriate, it is kind to offer to drop off a meal or to offer to help the grieving family with chores. Suffering the loss of a baby throws everything into chaos. Offering to help with light house cleaning or cooking or taking any other kids out for the afternoon is incredibly helpful. A very welcome gesture is a gift card to the family's favorite take out restaurant. When you are feeling over-whelmed, it's nice not to have to worry about prepping din-ner. It may not seem like much, but when you feel like you are drowning, help with the little things goes a long way. It is also something that is not intrusive and is always appreci-ated!

Things to Say (Deacon's Perspective)

Offer support and let the mother and family know you are there if they need something.

Sometimes the hardest thing in dealing with a tragedy is not becoming isolated. Now notice, this is different than needing to be alone. Isolation is when you intentionally sep-arate yourself from others, not so you can reconnect with God, recharge, or come back renewed; but specifically, so you can disconnect with God, continue in discouragement, and discharge yourself in your state of life. Isolation is a sign of desolation according to St. Ignatius of Loyola's Rules for Spiritual Discernment. Vinta Wright from Loyola Spiritual-ity Service tells us, "A person dwells in a state of desolation when she or he is moving away from God's active presence in the world."[1]

We want people to stay in the presence of God and so we want them to know the presence of God through being available for them. This means we must not be afraid to keep them in a state of consolation and away from desolation. If desolation moves us away from God, then its opposite consolation moves us towards Him.

Take Time to Notice
(Recognize signs of Consolation and Desolation)

This is particularly important for clergy, but also for friends. As clergy, we must recognize when people are being drawn away from God.

Signs of desolation (things that bring us away from God and the happiness we are made for) include:

- o Turning in on ourselves
- o Descending ever deeper into our own negative feelings
- o Cutting us off from community

---

[1] Vinta Wright. *Consolation and Desolation*. IgnatianSpirituality.com-A Service of Loyola Press. Accessed at: https://www.ignatianspirituality.com/consolation-and-desolation-2

- Making us want to give up on the things that used to be important to us
- Taking over our whole consciousness and crowding out our distant vision [this is despair]
- Covering up all our landmarks [the signs of our journey with God so far]
- Draining us of energy

Signs of consolation (things that keep us in the presence of God and on the path to the happiness we are made for) are:

- Directing our focus outside and beyond ourselves
- Lifting our hearts so that we can see the joys and sorrows of other people
- Bonding us more closely to our human community
- Generating new inspiration and ideas
- Restoring balance and refreshing our inner vision
- Showing us where God is active in our lives and where God is leading us
- Releasing new energy in us[2]

Note, that a Spiritual Director can help you take steps to stay on track with the path of consolation, but the community as a whole can help you to recognize when you are heading down the path of desolation. After all, "We are our

---

[2] Ibid.

brother's keeper" (Gen. 4:9) and so we must try to keep those who have experienced miscarriage or stillbirths on a safe path, a path filled with support and consolation.

DO:

Form groups that can address the financial, physical, and emotional support of the family.

After the loss of a baby the family may need help financially. There are many unexpected costs from funeral expenses to medical bills to loss of wages due to time missed from work. It's a blessing when a community rises to the occasion to assist families in the wake of loss. Families should embrace this community outreach and try to say "yes" as often as possible. Not only does it help the grieving family, but it also gives the community a sense of being helpful in being able to relieve some of the burden. Friends and family may also offer childcare, volunteer to do household chores, and offer general assistance which is also helpful for some families.

CLOSING THOUGHT FOR THIS PRESCRIPTION

In conclusion, we realize there are many things we CAN do or say, but that does not mean that we SHOULD do or say them. We offer these suggestions as a guide to help you know how to respond if you need help self-advocating after a loss or if you know someone who has recently suffered the loss of a baby. We hope these suggestions help you to do so effectively and with love!

Prescription 2

Care for the Mind (Psychology)

"Because you are precious in my eyes, and honored, and I love you"-Is. 43:4

Advice (Doctor's Perspective)

After experiencing a significant trauma like the loss of a baby, mothers are often thrown into resuming the daily routine of their lives without processing the trauma. Often miscarriages or stillbirths are accompanied by intense grief. However, this grief may turn into an actual medical condition such as depression or anxiety. They are both treatable disorders but often neglected. It is important for families to be aware of the difference between grief and depression. Something else important to point out is women who suffer early losses often do not get the intervention they need because they often do not participate in a burial, prayer service, meditative gathering, or memorial service, and so their loss is erroneously viewed as less worthy of long-term grief. We as a society fear death and grief and are wholly unprepared to cope when it occurs in our life. So, often, I work with patients on reframing their concept of grief. It won't stop the pain or sense of loss, but if we change how our brains inter-pret grief, we respond to it differently. I often hear patients talk about the five stages of grief and my advice is always the same: there is no roadmap for recovering from the death of a loved one. It looks differently for everyone; it is not linear. The goal is to reconceptualize the grief to introduce a new way forward so your mind is not trapped in a moment in time but is able to adapt to a life touched by loss.

There are many models of grief. Particularly noteworthy is the work of Dr. William Worden, a professor of psychol-ogy and expert on bereavement, and Dr. Colin Parkes, a well-known psychiatrist. In essence they both describe how to reframe and proactively address grief versus traveling through stages of grief. In their research, they suggest both processing and "retasking" the grief. When we are faced with the shock of loss, we would benefit from working towards accepting the reality of the loss. When we yearn for our loved one and feel that overwhelming pain of loss, then our "task" is to process the pain. When we eventually feel the despair and confusion often associated with the loss of a loved one, then our job is to adjust to the new reality and context of life without the person we lost. Finally, we reframe how the loss of the person impacts us and create a new vision for our life. This is a proactive approach to grief. It will give you back a sense of control over your grief, instead of feeling like grief controls you.

While the following is not meant to replace a consulta-
tion with a medical professional, it is important to be aware
of the various diagnosable and treatable conditions often associated with the loss of a child. The takeaway is to please,
please, please, seek professional help if you are feeling over-
whelmed with your loss. I cannot express this strongly
enough. In the case of depression, many families get confused by what they assume is an endless experience of grief.
Grief is very different from clinical depression. It is important for families to be aware of what the clinical symptoms of depression look like. If you or a loved one are experiencing any of these symptoms, it is very important to seek
treatment.

I often hear from patients, "I'm just sad. I'm not depressed. I'm not crazy!" ***Having a disorder like depression
or anxiety is in no way a reflection on whether you are sane
or not.*** After the loss of a baby, it is normal to feel many different emotions. However, sometimes, we cannot work
through them alone, and I strongly recommended working
with a psychologist or mental health professional to process
the traumatic experience of losing a baby.

<u>Depression</u>

Feeling "sad" after the loss of a child is normal. You have
experienced a significant trauma and unexpected loss. However, sometimes our grief spirals, and you can get "stuck,"

developing a depressive disorder. If you or a loved one is experiencing five or more of these symptoms within a two-week period and it represents a significant change from your previous state of functioning, please seek help from your doctor or a mental health professional.

1. **"I'm sad all the time"**

   It is perfectly natural to feel sad after experiencing a loss of this magnitude; however, if the sad mood continues and impairs functioning, this is considered an active symptom. This sadness is often all consuming and described as "trying to walk while carrying an elephant." It goes beyond "feeling blue;" it is a constant and unshakeable feeling of sadness that does not leave you.

2. **"I don't want to go"**

   Clinically this is known as anhedonia, and it is a term used to describe not wanting to engage in activities you used to enjoy. Things that used to make you happy, no longer have the same appeal. Patients often describe this symptom as "things just don't shine the way they used to, things don't taste the same, I just want to stay home and do nothing." Anhedonia is a common symptom for people suffering from depression. Going out and engaging with people or in activities, seems too overwhelming. This is a concept that has a spiritual parallel as well which

Deacon Anthony speaks of in the second part of this chapter.

3. **"I've gained or lost weight"**
    Depression is often accompanied by weight loss or weight gain (>5% in a month, either way). People often describe a significant increase in appetite that cannot be satiated or a loss of appetite.

4. **"I just want to sleep"**
    Another common symptom of depression is a noticeable change in sleeping patterns. Patients often report sleeping excessively (and not engaging in routine life activities) or getting less sleep than normal. This can also include "restless sleep" involving being able to fall asleep but waking up often. In this case you want to sleep but cannot. A patient once accurately described this experience as "my body desperately wants to sleep but I can't turn off my mind." On the other side of the coin are the patients who begin to sleep excessively. This becomes almost an avoidance of life because they feel so exhausted and "sleepy" they can no longer function effectively.

5. **"I have the jitters," or "I'm walking through quicksand all day"**
    Patients with depression sometimes describe a symptom of either feeling extremely restless or having significant

difficulty getting things done. People assume depression looks like the TV commercials where the person cannot get off the couch or pretends to hold up a smiley face, but in reality, the symptoms vary widely. While some do describe trying to climb a mountain while stuck in quicksand, as if they cannot get anything done, others describe feeling "jittery, agitated."

6. **"I can't adult today"**
    Have you ever felt really, really tired? Have you ever felt so tired that even physically putting on socks was too much? Patients with depression often share the symptom of extreme fatigue. However, it's not just the run of the mill tired. We are all tired! This is more like absolute exhaustion, like even the smallest task requires too much energy. It is not alleviated by rest or relaxation, it is constant.

7. **"It's my fault"**
    There is often an accompanying sense of guilt in patients with depression. Either directly or indirectly, patients with depression tend to blame themselves for feeling the way they do. They describe themselves as "weak" because they can't "snap out of it." Depression is a true medical condition. You cannot "snap" out of it any more than you can snap out of a broken bone. You can pray for the

strength to recover from a broken bone, but you still need a cast.

8. **"Mushy Brain"**
Patients with depression sometimes describe a symptom like "mushy brain." It's more than just being a little absent minded. There is a notable and observable change from previous functioning. Sometimes patients also report trouble making up their minds with even simple decisions. Others describe it as "brain fog:" trouble remembering things, trouble with task management and organization, and trouble focusing.

9. **"I wish I was dead"**
Depression can also be accompanied by recurrent thoughts of death. It's not just a fear of dying but in some cases wanting to die. This is a very serious symptom. If you have recurrent thoughts of death or wanting to die, don't try to check off five symptoms from the list, immediately seek help.

Depression looks different for everyone. It's the cluster of symptoms that determines whether it has reached a clinical level requiring intervention. Please do not think if you only have four of the five or three out of the five that you should not seek help. Child loss is traumatic and working with a mental health professional can help alleviate symptoms of depression and anxiety that often accompany trauma

Anxiety

Another common experience for mothers/families who have suffered child loss is the development of an Anxiety Disorder. Because child loss is usually so unexpected, it often triggers feelings you are not in control of your life. Many mothers (myself included) have described feeling anxious that something terrible would happen to our living children. One mother summed up the feeling quite well. She gave permission to share her story:

"I started having this irrational fear that my daughter (who was 2 at the time of my miscarriage) was going to die. She was perfectly healthy but I could not focus on anything but that something was also going to take her away. About a month after my miscarriage, she developed a cold, which became bronchitis. I was convinced she was dying of leukemia or some rare disease. I can't explain why I could not stop myself from spiraling. Even after her pediatrician assured me she was going to be okay, I had this awful nagging feeling. I started making up scenarios in my head. I had this awful panic every time she coughed. It was paralyzing, absolutely debilitating. I stayed up night after night researching symptoms, doctors, etc. Once the cough cleared up, then the fear became more generalized, that someone was going to abduct her, or she would fall at school and sustain a head injury. To this day I cannot explain why these thoughts kept popping in my head, but they resulted in daily panic attacks and constant fear. I didn't tell anyone and no one noticed at work because I kept functioning and, on the outside, it looked like I was holding it together. After three months of living this nightmare, a friend finally convinced me to see a psychologist. I was diagnosed with an anxiety disorder that had been exacerbated by the death of my baby. I had always been a bit anxious, but the miscarriage pushed me over the edge. It took a few months of therapy to finally start feeling like I was in control of my life again. I can honestly say the therapy saved my sanity and my relationship with my daughter."

Anxiety is also very common after the loss of a child. I personally experienced significant anxiety after the death of my twins. Like the mother above, I too had this irrational fear something was going to happen to my living son. Losing a child, especially unexpectedly, is like forever trying to catch your breath. It is difficult to feel steady when the world you had built is pulled out from under you. There is a loss of control after losing a child that generalizes to your other children, your family, your interpersonal relationships, your work, and your perspective on life. Imagine riding a roller coaster with a blindfold, without a seat belt, while running out of oxygen.

Below I share some diagnostic criteria for anxiety. As with depression, please do not try to self-diagnose and treat it. Use this as a guide. If you or a loved one can relate to these symptoms, seek help. Mental health is, sadly, still taboo in our society, but as I always say, if you break your arm, you aren't going to try to cast it yourself, are you? Seek professional help.

These are some symptoms of anxiety to look out for:

Nonstop Worry

We all have worries now and then, moments of apprehension, but excessive anxiety is when you experience feelings of tension or nervousness more days than not for at least six months. Think of this symptom as having a giant, terrifying spider attached to your back. This symptom is about actively worrying about anything and everything for more days out of your week than not.

Being Unable to Relax

This one infuriates me!! Have you ever had people tell you to just relax? When you have an anxiety disorder you can't control the worry. It's not a faucet you can turn off and on. The symptoms of anxiety do not just go away because you will them to, and you cannot just take a break from them when you would like to; I wish it were that easy. If you find it difficult to relax even when you are trying, that may be a symptom of anxiety.

Checklist

Have you experienced three or more of these symptoms for more days than not over a six-month period?

- Being easily fatigued, feeling worn out even when you aren't doing anything different from your normal routine.
- Difficulty concentrating or experiencing "memory fog," This is similar to a symptom of depression where you have trouble concentrating and perhaps have difficulty making decisions.
- Feeling anxious, "on edge," or restless. This symptom is often described as "feeling like your skin is crawling." It's also associated with being hypervigilant, always thinking something bad is going to happen.
- Being easily irritable. This one makes sense, doesn't it? If you are exhausted and constantly worrying, you are going to be cranky.
- Muscle aches. People often forget that physical symptoms are often part of mental health symptoms. Your brain and body are connected. If you are tense and unable to rest, your body will ache.

- Difficulty falling or staying asleep. Anxiety is often described as not being able to turn off your brain because it's going a mile a minute, creating worst case scenarios, and thinking of everything that can go wrong, etc. This is especially true at night!

If these symptoms are causing impairment in your life, it's time to talk to someone about them because you likely are experiencing clinical levels of anxiety.

Panic

There is a difference between panic attacks and panic disorder., Let's start with "what is a panic attack?"[3]

Clinical Definition of Panic Attacks:

"A panic attack is an abrupt surge of intense fear or intense discomfort that reaches a peak within minutes, and during which time four or more of the following symptoms occur":

---

[3] American Psychiatric Association. (2013). *Diagnostic and statistical manual of mental disorders* (5th ed.). https://doi.org/10.1176/appi.books.9780890425596. Text citation: (American Psychiatric Association, 2013).

1. "I'm having a heart attack" or "I think I'm having a stroke" describe the possible physical symptoms you may experience: like your heart is pounding or feeling like your heart is beating a mile a minute.

2. "I sweat a lot!" This symptom often manifests as excessive sweating in certain situations or night sweats. Sometimes the anticipation of having another panic attack triggers a panic attack. People may experience excessive sweat when in a triggering environment like a hospital or doctor's office or they wake up covered in sweat.

3. "My Hands shake!" Have you ever been so scared that you start to shake or your hands tremble? In a panic attack, people sometimes experience physical shaking and trembling.

4. "I can't breathe!" Shortness of breath is often a symptom associated with panic attacks.

5. "I can't swallow." Interestingly, another common symptom is feeling like "you have a lump in your throat", a sensation of having trouble swallowing.

6. "There's an elephant on my chest!" Chest pain is often reported as a symptom of a panic attack. Any chest pain should be taken seriously; seek medical treatment if you experience chest pain.

7. "I feel like my stomach is doing cartwheels." Feeling nauseous is a common symptom of a panic attack.

8. "I feel like the room is spinning." Feeling unsteady on your feet or feeling dizzy may also be experienced during a panic attack.

9. "Why is it so hot in here?" Temperature changes, such as feeling too cold or too hot without a medical cause can also be symptomatic of a panic attack.

10. "I'm here but I'm not here." This is described as a sense of detachment where you may be physically present, but not mentally or emotionally available.

11. "Everything is out of control." This is anticipatory fear of not being in control of your environment or decisions.

12. "I feel like I'm dying." During a panic attack, there are so many physical symptoms that people often worry they are actually dying of a heart attack or other condition.

At least one of the attacks has been followed by one or both of the following:

a. Constant worry about having another panic attack or associated symptoms

b. Noticeable change in response to being worried about having a panic attack or associated with the panic attacks.

Acute Stress Disorder

Acute Stress Disorder is a very common experience after the loss of a baby. The problem is we tend to think of trauma as more relevant to law enforcement and military personnel. However, the loss of a baby is traumatic. Acute Stress Disorder occurs after exposure to actual or threatened death or serious injury. This can be due to directly experiencing the traumatic event or witnessing the event as it occurred to others. In the case of child loss, the exposure to death is present. If you are also experiencing nine or more of the following from any of the categories below, you may be experiencing acute stress disorder and should seek treatment.

Intrusion Symptoms (unwelcome or uninvited)

- Repetitive, involuntary, and intrusive distressing memories of the traumatic event
    One mother describes this as "It just happens, I'm going about my day and a thought pops in about my baby, or about the funeral...I can't help it."
- Recurrent unwelcome dreams in which the content or impact of the dream are related to the traumatic event
- Dissociative reactions: These are colloquially known as "flashbacks". Many people have an unrealistic perception of what flashbacks look like. People describe

flashbacks as "relieving" part of the traumatic experience.

- Negative Mood: -this is more than just feeling sad. It
  is about a persistent negative head space, feeling like
  you are in a "dark place."

One patient describes her experience with flashbacks:

> "I remember getting up and going to work and when
> I heard an ambulance siren, I was suddenly 'reliving'
> my own experience in an ambulance when I lost the
> baby. It felt so real like I was there watching myself,
> like in a movie. I felt the chill of the winter air and the
> plastic of the gurney. And then after what seemed
> like an hour, I was sitting in my car. But I had no idea
> how I got there. It was terrifying."

Dissociative Symptoms (Inaccurate perception of reality or
of your surroundings, watching yourself as an outsider looking in, feeling as though you are in a daze, or experiencing
loss of time).

- Inability to remember an important aspect of the
  traumatic event. Sometimes patients describe "losing
  time" or having a gap in their memory of the traumatic event, almost as if their mind is trying to protect them from recalling the trauma.

- Avoidance symptoms-Think of this as not wanting to engage in activities, places, events, or people that may remind you of the traumatic event. This includes avoiding thinking about the event, thoughts, or feelings associated with the event. For example, not wanting to drive by the hospital where you had a D&C or avoiding baby showers.

Arousal Symptoms

- Sleep disturbance (Notice a trend? Sleep is really important and many psychological disorders impact sleep).
- Irritable behavior
- Hypervigilance- (Think of this as being "on watch" for something to go wrong, always expecting something bad to happen).
- Problems with concentration
- Exaggerated startle response (Sometimes after experiencing a trauma, you find yourself acting a bit more "jumpy" or quick to scare than prior to the trauma. For example, some moms describe a baby crying as terribly frightening after their loss).
- Duration of the symptoms is 3 days to 1 months after the trauma.
- Causes clinically significant distress or impairment to your daily functioning

- Acute Stress Disorder should resolve after one month. If it does not, then you may be looking at something more serious like an anxiety disorder or PTSD; absolutely consult a mental health professional.

Please use this as a guide to help you assess whether you need to seek help from your medical provider or a mental health care professional. As a clinical psychologist and also as a mother who has experienced child loss, please believe me when I say, sometimes you need professional support and guidance to process and survive such a significant loss.

Advice (Deacon's Perspective)

Doctor Heisman has just done a terrific job describing several psychological symptoms women may experience after a miscarriage or stillbirth. We especially know that sleep is an important indicator of our mental health. It is also an important indicator that we must not "sleep" on aiming to become the best-version of ourselves even amidst tragedy in life. This is why St. Paul tells us, "Do not be conformed to this world, but be transformed by the renewing of your minds, so that you may discern what is the will of God— what is good and acceptable and perfect" (Rom. 12:2).

In order to discern how to have our minds renewed (Christ's healing hands entering our psyche-good mental health), we must look at three basic spiritual principles explained by Fulton Sheen, himself a psychologist, pertaining to our encounter with good, evil and our psyche, which builds spiritual character.

In order to build character spiritually we must say "no" to something in order to get a fuller "yes". The athlete sometimes says no to ice cream so they can have a better run and their bodies can work more efficiently. A man says yes to one woman in marriage and in doing so he says no to every other woman on earth. Yes and no go together because expression (doing something) and repression (not doing something) are a natural part of growth, mending, and continuing in life. So, what do we say "yes" to and what do we say "no" to? There are three courses of action: Amputation, Mortification, and Limitation.[4]

Amputation refers to intrinsic evil (things that cannot be good in any circumstances).

Some examples of intrinsic evils are murder and adultery. Amputation means to completely cut off something and to disconnect it from the person including memory. We must be careful not to label the gestation of

---

[4] Fulton Sheen. *Life is Worth Living*: Character Building (San Francisco, CA: Ignatius Press, 1999), pp. 100-103. This section involving Amputation, Mortification, and Limitation are based on these pages.

our child and his/her memory as something we must separate ourselves from at all cost, analogous to an intrinsic evil; i.e., something that should be amputated and never remembered or thought about ever again. This is not spiritually or psychologically healthy because the gestation and memory of your child is NOT an intrinsic evil, but your child and the time of gestation is something that is very good.

Mortification refers to something that has a mix of both good and bad.

In mortification you suppress what is bad, but embrace what is good. Examples of mortification are fasting and almsgiving. Food is good, but you give it up so that you can grow spiritually and not make it the center of your life. As Fulton Sheen writes, "Dieting you give up food for the glory of self, fasting you give up food for the glory of God." In both, the good known as food is sacrificed for something higher, either self or God.

Relating this to child-loss, you must hold on to the good that is your child, the memories you have with your child, even if it is the memory of their growth inside of you or the bond that you have with the child through pregnancy. You may have to mortify and be aware of the painful memory of the loss of that child. You may have to come back to that memory however so that you can bring that into your life so you can encounter it and still live, rather than encounter it and want to flee.

Theologically, this is being able to "take up your cross [mortification] so you can follow Christ" (Lk. 9:23).

Limitation refers to those things that are simply good.

We must limit the good simply because of the fact that it is not God. If we do, we turn the icon (something that is meant to POINT us to God) into an idol (something that REPLACES God). This is the reason we have to limit the good things with the boundary that we take them in only as much as they can lead us to God. We must also limit it because too much of a good thing can harm us as we may not have the capacity to receive it. As John-Mark Miravalle notes, "Light [a good] doesn't only let you see; it can also blind you. So too, beauty can clarify things, and it can also make one appreciate the overwhelming depth of a mystery (as happens with Job at the end of his interaction with God)."[5]

You, like Job, have lost a child and it hurts because your child is a great good. However, the limiting of dwelling on losing your child and connecting it to the goodness of the child helps us to appreciate the

---

[5] John-Mark L. Miravalle. *Beauty: What it Is & Why It Matters* (Manchester, New Hampshire: Sophia Press, 2019), p. 34.

overwhelming depth of the mystery of life after the mis-carriage/stillbirth.

This means that you can take time to reminisce about your bond with the baby that you have lost through miscarriage or stillbirth, but you-cannot dwell on it to the point that it becomes the center of your life and you can no longer function. It's important to prudently judge how much time thinking about your beloved child is beneficial for you and how much time might start to blind you by preventing you from doing the other things that God has asked you to do in life.

We must decide on how to deal with good and bad things in life. We must decide if we will live in a state of amputation, mortification, and limitation in each good or bad aspect of life. We must also be able to properly discern between depression and spiritual darkness because they are often mistaken for one another because they have similar symptoms.

Just as you have to be careful when prescribing medication to someone who is coughing because coughing is a symptom for both Strep throat and choking, so too you must discern between depression (as mentioned in Dr. Heisman's section) and spiritual sorrow because how you apply the necessary "medicine" or procedure could mean the difference between life and death. Just as you wouldn't give antibiotics to someone who is choking, we must also not try to fix a spiritual problem with a psychological prescription or a psychological problem by telling someone to "just pray harder." Now to be clear, prayer is ALWAYS BENEFICIAL because grace builds on nature. On occasion we have to work on the natural so that it does not become a stumbling block to the supernatural. This means making our souls beautiful so they can have a spiritual glow, getting exercise and sleep so we can think clearly, seeking psychological help for anxiety or depression, all so God's grace can flow through us in a powerful way. Natural strengthening (such as good physical and mental health) can increase our ability to have supernatural docility and supernatural docility can help heal our nature. In other words, it is not either-or, but both; both must be strengthened by their proper means.

For example, when a baby dies through miscarriage or a stillbirth, parents may go into denial (the Spiritual and Emotional amputation we spoke of above). They want to forget the miscarriage or stillbirth so they can distance themselves from the heartache and pain. However, Dr. Aaron Kheriaty notes:

> The denial of death-or any other denial of reality-is indeed psychologically unhealthy; it is a type of delusional thinking, and we should not encourage it in our patients. I am convinced that all good psychotherapy rests on the premise that the truth is better than a lie, even when the truth is difficult or painful. While good psychotherapy can help cure our denial, it cannot solve the problem of

death's finality-nor should we expect it to. For these answers we turn to the science of reason (philosophy) and the science of faith (theology).[6]

Here are five general principles to discern the differences between depression and other mental health disorders and spiritual issues such as oppressive guilt, acedia/isolation, and spiritual purifications.

Principle 1: Miscarriage or stillbirth is NOT God punishing someone for their sins.

Oftentimes, in working with families, they try to "figure out" what they have done wrong to "deserve this." Tragedy, even death, is not simply due to the parents' sins, but for the glory of God who brings good out of even the greatest evil (death). We see this in the words of the Gospels themselves:

As he passed by, he saw a man blind from birth. His disciples asked him, "Rabbi, who sinned, this man or his parents, that he was born blind?" Jesus answered, "Neither he nor his parents sinned; it is so that the works of

---

[6] Aaron Kheriaty, MD and Fr. John Cihak, STD. *The Catholic Guide to Depression: How the Saints, the Sacraments, and Psychiatry Can Help You Break Its Grip and Find Happiness Again* (Sophia Institute Press: Manchester, New Hampshire, 2012), p. 159.

God might be made visible through him. We have to do the works of the one who sent me while it is day. Night is coming when no one can work. While I am in the world, I am the light of the world…. "Go wash in the Pool of Siloam" (which means Sent). So, he went and washed, and came back able to see. So, a second time they called the man who had been blind and said to him, "Give God the praise! We know that this man is a sinner." He replied, "If he is a sinner, I do not know. One thing I do know is that I was blind and now I see" (Jn. 9:1-5, 7, 24-25).

Sin can be a cause of punishment from a loving God that leads to repentance, BUT the death of a child is not something willed by God to teach parents a lesson.

This is the difference between God's direct will and His permissive will. In the direct will, God is the first cause of the action such as Inspiration of Scripture, giving of the Ten Commandments, and the Healing of the lepers. God is all-good, He "is light and in him there is no darkness at all" (1Jn. 1:5). Thus, He cannot act in an evil way because it would contradict His nature. The book of James emphasizes this point, "No one, when tempted, should say, "I am being tempted by God"; for God cannot be tempted by evil and he himself tempts no one" (Jas. 1:13). However, God can allow an evil to happen to bring about a greater good. This is God's permissive will. In summary, God's direct will can only do good because God can only act in a good way because something/someone must always act in accordance with its nature. God's permissive will allows evil or something bad to bring about a greater good. As the Gospel passage from John tells us, it is so "the works of God can be revealed in him." God continues to work, even amidst sorrow. The work of God is love and God continues to love **us and the baby** He has taken to Himself, especially while we are experiencing grief.

This brings us to a crucial point. Suffering and grief are transformed by the Cross of Jesus Christ. The entire point of life is "Communion with God" because that is the nature of love; to be present with the beloved. Because of sin, and thus our fallen natures; our wills, intellects, and emotions have been twisted so that life events can take us away from God rather than bring us closer to Him. But because Christ has conquered sin, death, and sorrow by His death on the cross, death and sorrow can now actually be transformed into a means of uniting even closer to God the Father. This is the reason people have a devotion to Our Lady of Sorrows. At the foot of the Cross, the death of her Son Jesus Christ, is where Mary was brought to her deepest communion with God the Father through the Holy Spirit. God calls us through sorrow and joy, at the manger and the crucifixion; in times of starvation (multiplication of the loaves and fishes-Mk. 6:30-44) and great feasts (Last Supper-Matt. 26:26-30). God calls us in all events to a deeper Communion with Him and this has a tremendous meaning in our lives, especially in dealing with death. Fr. Cihak tells us:

> The person suffering from depression needs to know and to recall this, the deepest of truths: he or she is not alone. Christ is there in the darkness; in our pain, as in our joy, we can be united to Christ. Christian revelation, therefore, leads to freedom from sorrow of total despair and dejection, and yet acknowledges a salutary sorrow producing repentance and union with God...The person suffering from depression may also be experiencing a participation in the agony of the Cross.[7]

God can call us to Himself through sorrows and joy, sickness and in health, in good times and in bad giving us a blueprint for spousal accompaniment. As the prophet Isaiah would write:

> For your husband is your Maker;
> the LORD of hosts is his name,
> Your redeemer, the Holy One of Israel,
> called God of all the earth. (Is. 54:5).

God is our Immanuel; He is with us (Matt. 1:23). This is the fulfillment of the Beatitude, "Blessed are they who mourn,

---

[7] *Catholic Guide to Depression*, p.55.

for they will be comforted." (Matt. 5:4). Erasmo Leiva-Meri-
kakis shares a great insight into this:

> The follower of Jesus in the Beatitudes is hopeful
> within sorrow and grief, even if he is tempted to des-
> pair. He is hopeful because Jesus is there with him. The
> phrase "shall be comforted" literally means, "to be called
> to someone's side." The sorrowful are called close to Je-
> sus' side; they are not abandoned…" God does not con-
> sole us by abolishing our solitude but by entering it and
> sharing it." The disciple of Christ has a hopeful sorrow
> because Jesus is with him. And this hopeful sorrow-this
> sorrow of love-is indeed a Christian virtue.
>
> All suffering is relativized by his love. Suffering is
> compelled by Christ to become a grammar of his love.
> No suffering or misery is greater than God; depression
> need not utterly overwhelm those who are united to him.
> Instead of indicating separation from God, suffering can
> become a vehicle by which one is brought into deep inti-
> macy with him. Human suffering can have sanctifying
> value when united to the sufferings of Christ. For the first
> time since the Fall, the human race does not have to be
> irredeemably sad. We need not give in to despair. One of
> the first consequences of the Cross and Resurrection is
> that the disciple is freed from oppressive sorrow.[8]

---

[8] *Catholic Guide to Depression*, pp. 51, 53.

There is a difference between various kinds of sorrow, which brings us to our next principle.

Principle 2: There is a difference between spiritual sorrow, psychological depression, and oppressive sorrow.

Spiritual Sorrow

Sorrow that results from guilt due to sin or contact with evil. It is there to help a person turn away from sin or evil and back towards God. Refer back to the paragraph explaining God's direct versus God's permissive will.

Our goal is to be in communion with God. God does this not to be cruel, but because He loves us. The Lord permits sorrowful events to bring us closer to Him as a disciple must imitate his teacher. Our Lord, "Although he was a Son, ...learned obedience through what he suffered; and having been made perfect, he became the source of eternal salvation for all who obey him" (Heb. 5: 8-9). If our Lord was made perfect through what he suffered, we too must follow his example as his disciples. Thus, the book of Hebrews continues, "Now, discipline always seems painful rather than pleasant at the time, but later it yields the peaceful fruit of righteousness to those who have been trained by it (Heb. 12:11). We can be trained by sorrow. It can deepen and strengthen our roots. St. Margaret Mary Alacoque tells us this beautifully,

"Look upon yourself as a tree planted beside the water, which bears its fruit in due season; the more it is shaken by the wind, the deeper it strikes its roots into the ground." This type of sorrow brings about the good fruits of repentance, turning away from sin and evil, and union with God, which is turning towards God's mercy and love.

Oppressive Sorrow

Sorrow that separates someone from God. It gets its name from something external, i.e., not internal, enslaving or binding someone to something that is not good for them. When the Devil uses objects to keep someone from God, it is called diabolical oppression Note: This is NOT saying that someone who has oppressive sorrow needs an exorcism, this is simply giving the background to the definition of the word.

However, spiritual sorrow is different from oppressive sorrow and depression. Oppressive sorrow is sorrow that is fruitless and simply embitters a person. This is the sorrow that separates someone from God. So oppressive sorrow can happen after the loss of a baby, when a person embraces atheism and separates him or herself from God. Note, this does not mean you cannot express your emotions with God, He wants to hear from you in both good times and in bad, but He does not want you to choose to separate from Him.

Depression can become oppressive sorrow, but it is not inevitable. Once again Fr. Cihak explains:

> When one is depressed, it is important to remember that God's presence in the soul is an objective fact, which is not dependent on our subjective state or our interior experiences...No form of interior suffering or pain-no matter how acute and distressing-can erase this objective fact. God does not abandon us; it is only we, by our willful and deliberate sins [that is choosing to separate ourselves from God], who abandon him.[9]

Oppressive sorrow comes when we choose to allow our sorrow or depression to separate us from God.

Depression in and of itself is not a sin. To sin, you must have full knowledge something is wrong, you willingly choose to do it anyway, and depending on whether it is serious matter depends on whether it is mortal or venial (see *Catechism of the Catholic Church* #1857). Depression can be caused by things beyond our control such as chemical imbalances in the brain, traumatic life experiences, some temperaments are more prone to depression than others. For example, melancholics are more likely to have depression than a sanguine. Other causes of depression are lack of sleep or nutrition, and even through weather-related triggers such as

---

[9] *Catholic Guide to Depression*, p.76.

in Seasonal Affective Disorder. You may be down during those long winter months, but that does not mean your depression has to separate you from God. In fact, going through bouts of depression can actually bring you closer to God and so can become heroic virtue.

St. Jane Francis de Chantel is one example of many saints who demonstrate this.[10] She struggled with depression which was triggered by the death of her husband. But she did not let death take her away from God even though it was a life-long struggle. Through her depression, she found a great spiritual director named St. Francis de Sales, entered into religious life, and founded the Order of Visitation nuns whom our Lord would appear to reveal devotion to His Sacred Heart through St. Margaret Mary Alacoque. Could it possibly be that this devotion was the good fruit of St. Jane Chantal's perseverance and sanctification of her depression? God knows and He wants us to know that even if we do have depression, it does not have to lead to leaving Him. It can lead to perseverance, virtue, and a more intimate relationship with the God who loves us.

---

[10] Meg Hunter-Kilmar. Aleteia. *Saints Who Battled Mental Illness*. May 16, 2020. Accessed at: https://aleteia.org/2020/05/16/saints-who-battled-mental-illness.

Principle 3: Healing Does not Mean you will never have sorrow.

Jesus tells us, "Amen, amen, I say to you, you will weep and mourn, while the world rejoices; you will grieve, but your grief will become joy. So, you also are now in anguish. But I will see you again, and your hearts will rejoice, and no one will take your joy away from you" (Jn. 16: 20, 22). He speaks of the pain, but that pain being transformed into joy when Jesus sees us again. When we are in communion with Him no one can take that joy away from us. Nothing can take us from the love of Christ! This is the reason St. Paul writes in his letter to the Romans:

> What then shall we say to this? If God is for us, who can be against us? What will separate us from the love of Christ? Will anguish, or distress, or persecution, or famine, or nakedness, or peril, or the sword? No, in all these things we conquer overwhelmingly through him who loved us. For I am convinced that neither death, nor life, nor angels, nor principalities, nor present things, nor future things, nor powers, nor height, nor depth, nor any other creature will be able to separate us from the love of God in Christ Jesus our Lord (Rom. 8:31, 35, 37-39).

Nothing can separate us from the love of Christ, but that does not mean that we will not have sorrow or trouble in this

life. Jesus tells us the exact opposite, "I have told you this so
that you might have peace in me. In the world you will have
trouble, but take courage, I have conquered the world" (Jn.
16:33). **Healing does not mean an absence of sorrow. Healing means going forward, even amidst sorrow, with and in
Jesus Christ/God.**

Fulton Sheen gives us great insight into this. Going forward depends on how you view your pain. He writes as follows: [11]

> There are two ways of looking at [pain]; one is to see
> it without purpose, the other is to see it with pur-
> pose…The way we will react to pain depends entirely
> upon our philosophy of life. As the poet has put it:
>
> Two men looked out through their prison bars;
>   The one saw mud, the other stars….
>
> These two attitudes are manifested in the two thieves
> crucified on either side of Our Blessed Lord. The thief on
> the right is the model for those for whom pain has a
> meaning; the thief on the left is the symbol of unconse-
> crated suffering.

---

[11] Fulton J. Sheen. *Go to Heaven: A Spiritual Roadmap to Eternity* (San Francisco, CA: Ignatius Press, 2017), pp. 212-216.

Consider first the thief on the left. He suffered no more than the thief on the right, but he began and ended his crucifixion with a curse...Because he could not assimilate his pain and make it turn to the nourishment of his soul, pain turned against him as a foreign substance taken into the stomach turns against it and infects and poisons the whole system. That is why he became bitter, why his mouth became a crater of hate, and why he cursed the very Lord Who could have shepherded him into peace and paradise. The world today is full of those, who like the thief on the left, see no meaning in pain. Knowing nothing of the redemption of the Lord, they are unable to fit pain into a pattern; it becomes just an odd patch on the crazy quilt of life...The lesson of the thief on the left is clear: pain of itself does not make us better, it is apt to make us worse...Unspiritualized suffering does not improve man; it degenerates him. The thief at the left is no better for his crucifixion: it sears him, burns him, and tarnishes his soul....

Now look at the thief on the right-the symbol of those for whom pain has meaning. Pain began to be comprehensible to the thief...Pain was dropping scales away from his eyes; and, turning toward the central cross, he no longer saw a crucified man, but a heavenly King.... Pain in itself is not unbearable; it is the failure to understand its meaning that is unbearable. If the thief did not see the purpose in pain, he would have never saved his soul. Pain can be the death of our soul, or it can be its life…. Pain is sacrifice without love. Sacrifice is pain with love.

The question is what do we keep in our hearts while being on the cross of miscarriage and stillbirth and which thief do we embrace? Do we hold *unspiritualized suffering or pain* in our hearts and thus embrace the thief on the left allowing him to steal our joy, peace, and serenity? Or do we make a *sacrifice* in our hearts, connect pain with purpose, which allows healing to take place. Thus, embracing the thief on the right allowing him to steal our pain, confusion, anger, and instability so we can unite that sacrifice of our hearts to the cross of Christ. Let us aim to turn all of our pain into sacrifices so this way it is always united to love, and thus to God.

Principle 4: Depression/Anhedonia versus Acedia/Isolation

The fourth principle involves distinguishing between the emotions of sadness which in a chronic state can lead to the clinical diagnosis of depression/anhedonia, and the choice of acedia/isolation (a spiritual sin). It is important because both depression/anhedonia and Acedia can lead to isolation which are one of the tools that can separate us from God's love. Emotions are morally neutral in and of themselves. They are data points. It is what we do with those emotions that can turn us to sin. Sadness is an emotion that comes about when we sense an evil (absence of a good). It encourages us to flee from the evil, but when we cannot flee the evil, it can lead to despair. These emotions can paralyze us and thus everything in our lives can suffer including our time with God.

Acedia/Isolation (sometimes called sloth) is described by Fr. Peter John Cameron, O.P as "sadness about what ought to gladden us most: participation in the very life of God. This paralysis cutting us off from God is not an external obstacle but an interior one."[12] After the loss of the baby a mother may slowly become stronger emotionally and socially but when it comes time to pray, she allows her spouse to lead. Acedia is a slowness and repulsiveness, even eventual isolation, involving the things of God. Depression involves a slowness in all aspects of life, but acedia involves a slowness and/or isolation in the Spiritual aspects of life. Many moms can sink into acedia because they think "God has hurt me by taking away my baby so I'll hurt Him by giving Him the silent treatment." A mom may be slow to talk with the Lord, but the irony is that the very God who is love, (1Jn. 4:8) who can help her move forward, is the very person she is choosing to keep seldom company. This can happen with dads too, but

---

[12] Fr. Peter John Cameron, O.P. Catholic Education Resource Center. *The Noonday Devil: Acedia.* Accessed online at https://www.catholiceducation.org/en/religion-and-philosophy/spiritual-life/acedia-30-06-17.html

usually because of the physical, hormonal, and emotional bond with the baby mothers experience this more frequently.

One way to determine if someone is dealing with depression or acedia is by examining what the person wants to avoid. If the person wants to avoid people, activities, and the ordinary things of life; it may be depression. If the person wants to avoid their vocation such as avoiding the things involving their marriage like spousal and family obligations, which is God's chosen path for their lives, it is acedia. If a person wants to avoid Communion with God, prayer, or going to Church; that also is acedia. Acedia wants to avoid all the things that will bring her or him into contact with God. The person who has depression just wants to avoid life in general.

Principle 5: Spiritual Purification versus Depression

A few women have approached me about experiencing the Dark Nights of Sense and Soul. I wanted to take a few pages to explain these Dark Nights also known as spiritual purifications in order for someone to determine if spiritual direction is part of your individual prescription for healing. Please know this section is not an all-encompassing way to solve the spiritual need of advice to get through spiritual purifications, but it is a good start to give you some benchmarks to look for in your spiritual life. If this does not refer to you at the present moment you can jump ahead to Prescription 3, but I encourage you to read it as all people have to go through these purifications eventually to be made whole and be prepared for the love of Heaven.

We have to have the senses and soul purified because things of the flesh, also known as the body depending on the emphasis of spiritual life or the actual body's operation such as feeling and emotion, and disorders of the soul can keep us from taking flight:

> Therefore, St. John of the cross tells us, there are many good things here on earth, but they are not God. He is not saying, "Love God instead of people or other things, but love them correctly in God." …
>
> So, through this painful purification, we come to realize that as good as God's gifts are, they are not meant to be ends in themselves. We learn to love God and realize that if we love the Giver, He will freely give us His gifts as well. In this, we will have reached the side of Christ. At this point we can start to see that we are no longer servants of our passions and desires, but are their master. In this, we learn that God loves us and is calling us to more. So let us not be content with coming to the side of Christ, but fulfill our concrete possibilities, as

John Paul II speaks of, to be the beloved of God; see Him face to face. Thus, we travel into the Illuminative Stage.[13]

Having your senses purified so that they lead you to God and not simply to self (the ego), nor the Biblical meaning of the world as one of the three temptations that lead away from God, can be painful. The pain is magnified when the faculties of the soul have to be purified as well. These faculties are your intellect, memory, and will. Each of these are directed towards the three theological virtues which unite us closer to God: Faith, Hope, and Love. Your intellect involves Faith, your memory involves Hope, and your will involves Love. All of these must be purified because we have a pseudo-version of these virtues but they must be made into the real thing so we can dwell with God in truth:

> The intellect is purified by obtaining true faith. If you really think about it, much of what we deem as faith is based on reason. We believe what the Church teaches because it makes sense. It makes sense that Christ would set up a Church. We believe in Christian morals because we can see that it makes the world a better place. This isn't true faith because true faith "is the realization of what is hoped for and evidence of things not seen" (Heb. 11:1).

---

[13] Gerard-Marie Anthony. *Who Am I: The Theology of the Body in Prayer* (Waterford, MI: Bezalel Books, 2011), pp. 63-64.

In this part of the purification, all the constructs that held up your faith are taken away. It's not that the faith will no longer make sense, but you will have this yearning like, "Is it all real?" It is what is equivalent to getting cold feet before the wedding night. We can begin to think to ourselves, "What if he or she really doesn't love me?" We must have faith. It is like that famous saying on the Eucharist, "For those who believe, no explanation is necessary; for those who do not believe, no explanation is possible." In the end you believe simply because you trust in God.

The memory is purified through true Hope. We have hope because we can visibly see all the things that God has given us: a roof over our head, food to eat, life, people, friends, family, and talents. Our memory is filled with these many gifts we have received, and we think that we deserve all these great gifts or those we have "earned them for ourselves." ... God through this purgation takes away this sensation and we realize that we don't have anything except for what God gives us.... This is true hope. Trusting that God will give us everything we need for heaven **freely** and it is not us earning our way to it (heaven).

The will is purified through true Love. Most of us love God because we can feel He loves us back. In this purgation, we lose the "feeling of God's love" and must love Him even though it feels like He has completely abandoned us. Through this purgation, we learn what real love is because we learn to love the same way God loves us. Think about it, God loves us not because he needs us or because he gets something out of it. He brought us into being out of love, not obligation. We, on the other hand, mostly love God out of obligation. He actually loves us even when we insult him, deny him, and try to run from him. Just look at the cross. God loves us even when we're unlovable and we are called to love in this same way... Try this with the hard to get along with co-worker or the homeless man at the soup kitchen. This is loving with God's love. God uses this purification so we can be tested to see if we will love God this way. If we love Him even if He gives us nothing. The irony is the more we love Him for Himself, the more He will shower us with His gifts. ***Throughout this time of feeling of complete abandonment, we come to realize the more we strive to dwell in God, the more He's there all along. Just look at the Stations of the Cross. God never takes the cross away from Jesus, but He does send someone to be with him every step of the way.*** Thus, we see that our souls in their intellect, will, and memory are purified through faith, hope, and love... We have been enlightened to how much God truly loves us and who we are as persons.

Thus, we enter into the final stage, the Unitive Stage.[14]

The Unitive Stage is the stage in which we are united in every way to God except for eternity. We are all called to this stage because all of us are called to the heights of love. The two purifications of the Senses and the Soul help us to get there. Both purifications can look like depression, but in actuality they are something completely different. Dr. Kheriaty gives some great differences between the Dark Nights and Depression:

> Depression involves the loss of ordinary abilities to function mentally and physically, and it can also be triggered by interpersonal loss, loss of a job, and so forth. The interior dryness of the dark night of the senses involves a loss of pleasure in the things of God and in some created things. However, it does not involve disturbed mood, loss of energy (cognitive or motor slowing), or diminished sexual appetite -all of which are seen commonly in depression. Those in the dark night of the senses have trouble applying their mental faculties to the practice of prayer and meditation,

---

[14] *Who Am I: The Theology of the Body in Prayer*, pp. 82-84.

but do not typically have difficulty concentrating
or making decisions in other areas of life.

With the dark night of the spirit...there is an acute
awareness of one's own unworthiness before God, of
one's personal defects and moral imperfections, and of
the great abyss between oneself and God. However, a
person in this state does not experience morbid thoughts
of excessive guilt, self-loathing, feelings of utter worth-
lessness, or suicidal thoughts-all of which are commonly
experienced during a depressive episode. Furthermore,
neither of the two dark nights involves changes in appe-
tite, sleep disturbances, weight changes, or other physical
symptoms (e.g., gastrointestinal problems, chronic pain)
that sometimes accompany depression.[15]

It is important to distinguish between these two as I have
seen many people going through clinical depression who
think they are going through a spiritual purification (usually
Dark Night of the Senses because they are basing it on their
emotions) and thus think they can just pray away their depression. They will do hours of prayers, rosaries, and nove-
nas but will never get psychological treatment. Of course,
God can work miracles, but God also works through the ordinary means He has set before us. In these cases, it is better

---

[15] *Catholic Guide to Depression*, p. 66-67

to consult a psychiatrist or psychologist. On the other hand, there are some people who are being purified spiritually and keep running to counseling, but their counselor can't help them because it is a matter of grace at work so a Spiritual Director is the ordinary means that God would use to heal in these situations.

Depression united with grace can have some of the same effects as the Spiritual purifications. Parker Palmer explains this in a mind-blowing way:

> Depression has taught me that there is something far deeper in me and stronger and truer than my ego, my emotions, my intellect, or my will. All of these faculties have failed me in depression, and if they were all I had, I do not believe I would still be here to talk about the experience. Deeper down there is a soul...that helps explain (for me, at least) where the real power in life resides.[16]

This teacher and writer embraced his Dark Night of the Senses by reflecting on his depression! In him, we can see how grace truly does build on nature and how each complement one another. His experience with therapy enabled him to get to the point where his mind was docile enough to turn to prayer and meditation. In return, that prayer and

---

[16] *Catholic Guide to Depression*, p. 193.

meditation purified his senses so he could realize that there was something deeper than his ego or just what he wanted.

Thus, to conclude the Deacon's view in psychology (I jokingly say, "I'm not a psychologist or counselor, but only play one on tv"), let us remember the three courses of action we have to interact with evil or difficult situations: Amputation, Mortification, and Limitation. Then let us remember these five general principles to discern between psychology and spirituality so we can have the right doctors prescribing the correct medicine to make us whole:

- The miscarriage or stillbirth is NOT a punishment from God for sin.
- There are differences between spiritual sorrow, psychological depression, and oppressive sorrow.
- **Healing does not mean you will never have sorrow.**
- We must distinguish between the emotions of sadness (in a chronic state can lead to the clinical diagnosis of depression) and the choice of acedia (a spiritual sin).
- We must also distinguish between Spiritual Purifications and Depression.

Prescription 3

Questions about the Body's Response to Miscarriage/Still birth (Medical)

"The Lord created medicines out of the earth, and the sensible will not despise them"-Sirach 38:4 (NRSVCE)

Doctor's Perspective

There are so many things I did not know about the medical process and subsequent experience of having a miscarriage. And once you are in the middle of one, it is not practical to try and research what is happening. You are already confused by what is happening, and there is so much new medical terminology that the entire process is destabilizing. Even being in the medical field, I was confused and angry at some of the terms used. For example, in the hospital as I was waiting for my D& C (Dilation and Curettage) and asking to make sure they saved my babies' remains so we could bury them, the doctor kept using the term "fetal tissue" to describe my babies. Even after asking them to please use the term baby when describing my child, the staff said, "oh, it's too small to bury, we usually just dispose of it in the biohazard waste." That did not go over well and needless to say, everyone got an earful about respecting our views on human life and remains no matter the size. But it is a good example because you will hear so many different descriptions of what your body is going through depending on which stage of pregnancy you were in when you suffered the loss.

In a first trimester miscarriage, terms like anembryonic gestation, fetal demise, embryonic demise, incomplete abortion, inevitable abortion, missed abortion, and spontaneous abortion are common. It was incredibly confusing at first because my hospital paperwork (after the doctor failed to completely remove my babies in the first D&C), read "missed spontaneous abortion." I called the hospital very upset saying I didn't have an abortion; I had a miscarriage. The nurse very gently explained it is a medical term used when a miscarriage occurs. While it may seem irrational, it felt as though the paperwork was implying it was a choice that I made to end my pregnancy. It was an added stressor I could have done without.

There are things you will need to decide during a miscarriage. Sometimes, you will be in so much shock that you will have trouble processing what the doctor is saying. And sometimes, they tend to talk fast because it is so common for them, which of course is in no way comforting. Some options during miscarriage include: doing nothing and seeing if nature will take its course at home, surgical intervention like a D&C, and medication management to induce the process. All have different risk factors. In some cases, doing nothing might lead to greater complications in the long term with excessive bleeding and if you are past 10 weeks, you may not have this option. This was the case in my pregnancy. I opted for a D&C because the babies were too large to pass naturally but too small for inducing labor. The D&C is quick and done under what they call "MAC anesthesia" or "monitored anesthesia," which is considered a "light dose," and the procedure takes about 15 minutes. It is associated with some risks as any procedure is but usually includes only mild bleeding and cramping. Finally, there's medication that you can take which will jumpstart the process of your uterus contracting and expelling the remains. There is no right answer except to talk to your doctor about all your options, and if you are not comfortable, get a second and third opinion.

First trimester miscarriages are the most common and account for about 80% of losses during the first trimester (800,000 documented according to the CDC). As the weeks of the pregnancy continue, the chances of loss are reduced. From a medical perspective, a stillbirth occurs when a baby dies in the womb after 20 weeks gestation. Most research states loss after 20 weeks, relatively low at 1-3% or about 24,000-25,000 babies a year. That doesn't sound low to me!

Usually, stillbirths are delivered by either inducing labor, performing a dilation and evacuation (D&E) similar to the D&C previously discussed, or by C-section. All of these are often very traumatic for the mother and family. Not only do you go through the pain of childbirth, but at the end you do not get to take your baby home. Again, each course of action has benefits and risks, so discuss all options with your healthcare provider to make sure you understand each option and are ultimately comfortable with your decision. One patient described her experience with stillbirth:

> "I knew my baby had died at 30 weeks. I knew because I endured multiple sonograms, ultrasounds, etc., all confirming there was no hope. But as I sat in the hospital with nurses and doctors quietly sticking an IV needle into me, hooking me to monitors, there was a small part of me that kept hoping they were all wrong. That somehow my baby was alive and it was all one big mistake. I thought if I just endure the agonizing pain of childbirth, then my reward would be to hold my beautiful, living, breathing baby. I don't know why I thought this, maybe it was some way to protect myself from what was about to happen. When the baby came out, I kept waiting for it to cry. I was so confused. At one point I even asked, "is it okay?" The doctors and nurses were kind. I was terrified to hold the baby, but they said I should. The baby wasn't scary. He was beautiful. I don't know if it made it better or worse. I do treasure the pictures I have of him. I just remember all the pregnant mothers I saw on the way out who got to leave with their babies in their arms. It was all so traumatic. I'm in therapy now, my husband and I both are, and I don't know if we will get past this or how anyone survives this, but we are trying."

In many ways it feels cruel, no matter in which stage of pregnancy the loss occurred, to still feel pregnant after the loss. That is something else many women do not expect and are not prepared for. Each experience with child loss is unique, as are our bodies. Many women still feel pregnant after a loss. That's perfectly normal. Hormones are still dysregulated and our physical and psychological connection to our babies is still very strong.

Other experiences during a miscarriage and stillbirth include: bleeding, cramping, muscle pain, and nausea. Our bodies and our minds are connected. Give yourself permission to listen to your body. Sometimes we have to be our own medical advocates. Let's be honest, we've all experienced a medical appointment where we felt unheard or rushed. If something does not feel right, do not hesitate; advocate for yourself and your child. Sometimes, we don't get any physical warnings that something is wrong. I had no idea my child's heart had stopped beating when I went in for a routine checkup. But to this day, I wish I had asked more questions about everything that came after the loss. The doctors and nurses just kept repeating how common miscarriages are and that I could try again. And don't get me wrong, there were so many wonderful and compassionate doctors and nurses throughout the process. But no system is perfect, and professionally speaking, we as health professionals are often exhausted! Each patient, each baby is special and should be treated with respect and kindness. Ask as many questions as you need to feel comfortable with your decision.

There is another medical concept I would like to share which mothers have found helpful after suffering a miscarriage. The concept is microchimerism. When a woman is pregnant, fetal cells belonging to the baby travel from the baby to the mother. Interestingly, even after the birth or loss of a child, the baby's cells may remain within the mother for an extended time. While initial studies suggest that microchimerism may have both beneficial and adverse effects for the mother, grieving mothers may be comforted to know that a physical, tangible part of their child remains within their bodies long after pregnancy. One of the most distressing aspects of miscarriage and stillbirth is that you often don't have anything physical to remember the baby except sonogram pictures or a grave. It was incredibly comforting to know that my babies' cells were still inside me and that I keep a piece of them with me. It may not sound like much to an outside observer, but it sometimes provides a tremendous source of comfort for a grieving mother.

Deacon's Perspective

Pope Saint John Paul II had a beautiful teaching called the Theology of the Body. In it, he proposes the great teaching that our bodies actually can teach us something about God, our dignity, and our worth. Let's take for example a

Prescription 4

Unlocking God's Perspective (Spiritual Aspects)

"See, I am sending an angel before you, to guard you on the way and bring you to the place I have prepared."
- Exodus 23:20.

Deacon's Perspective

We've looked at prescriptions concerning psychology and medicine, and now we come to the spiritual/pastoral prescription. This is a powerful dose of medicine because we all have a connection to our creator and are religious by nature. Thus, this prescription involves something fundamental to our humanity. There are six big areas that we must focus on with this prescription especially when we have questions about God and the Church's role in situations involving loss. We can address these questions by remembering to A.S.K H.I.M!

Approach God with the tough questions
See God in Truth
Know you and your family's dignity and worth

Help: Accompaniment vs Abandonment

Information -Canon Law, Order of Christian Funerals, and Catechism of the Catholic Church

Making the Church Community aware and forming support

Each of these areas are crucial in the spiritual response to the loss of a child so let us start to examine each part of the prescription.

Approach God with the tough questions

This is a fundamental first step because oftentimes we have questions but will not be at peace until we do something with those questions. Science often answers the question "how" or "what"? We may understand "what" happened during a miscarriage and even "how" it came about, but there are still some especially important questions which only religion answers. Religion answers the question "why?" and contrary to what we may think, Jesus wants us to ask this question! Why did this happen? Why did this have to happen to me? Why do I feel like there's something wrong with me? Why do I feel guilty...ashamed...like it's my fault? All of these are important questions and may be part of someone's healing. Hence, Jesus tells us, "Ask and you shall receive, seek and you shall find, knock and the door will be opened to you" (Matt. 7:7).

If we dare to come to God and His Church with the tough questions, we may not get all the answers, at least this side of Heaven, or even the answers we are looking for, but we then allow ourselves to get enough information to continue another day. Sometimes God gives us "our daily bread" (Matt. 6:11) and other times he gives us "a new heart" (Ez. 11:19). Either way, He gives us these often on the condition that we approach Him and ask to be fed or transformed.

See God in Truth

We must **"See God in Truth."** After approaching God, this is the second most important step because it allows us to have the courage to continually approach God. You will not approach someone if you fear that person. God wants you to approach Him and receive the blessings/grace He wishes to give us during these times of trial and beyond. We must see God in truth because the way we see God will affect how we receive His answers. Let us look at some real-life examples and then see how they are parables for how we view God just as Jesus used the Story of the Prodigal Sons in Luke 15 for the same purpose. Be patient and reflect as to which one might be how you view God.

The first example is dealing with a boss who seems to always be a jerk and you want to ask him for a raise to help better your life. You walk in and ask for the raise, and your boss starts off with, "No…". Because you view your boss as a jerk and a constant source of frustration, you may just walk out the office or tune out everything he says afterwards.

Another example is if you are going through a tough time in life and you get stranded in a parking lot because your car battery dies. You are trying to get through to your husband and he won't pick up his phone. After the fifth time calling, you get frustrated thinking he is ignoring your calls because the football game is on which always seems to be more important. While you are stuck in the parking lot, your neighbors drive by and sees you stranded and so tells the husband when they get back to the house that his wife needs help. The husband calls you back after your sixth time calling and says hello, but you just unload on him because he was not there for you in your time of need.

A third example is a teenage child who comes up to her dad and tells him "Good morning." You can more or less tell when something is going on with your kids. The dad can tell there was something wrong and she was visibly shaken. So, he asks her to sit down and then says, "Is everything alright?" After a few seconds of gathering herself she says to him with a tear in her eye, "I accidentally ran over the mailbox on the way from school." Then the dad gives her a great big hug, asks if she's hurt, and then because she is scared, the dad sacrifices some of his sleep to drive with her to keep her calm until she gets confidence to drive again.

All three of these are analogies of how we can view God during the time of miscarriage. The first example is seeing

God like this boss or taskmaster who is always asking us to follow rules, to give more, but never gives us what we want (even if it is the gift of a child). It seems like He just said no to something that would be beneficial to both of us. In this example, we may be tempted to try to walk away or block out what He is trying to tell us. We might be tempted to quit, leave Him and become part of "a different company" of non-believers? In the second example, we can see God as someone who didn't answer or continues to ignore our prayers; we see Him from a Deist perspective meaning He creates us but then abandons us. We think we are on our own so we don't really want to talk to Him when He "finally gets back to us." Finally, there's the third example which is an example of a loving father who cares for his daughter. Which of these is the True God? This is a crucial question because truth is defined as when our minds match up with reality. [17] If Jesus tells us, "I am the way, the truth, and the life" (Jn. 14:6) and we are going to continue forward in life, we must determine the truth about God! Is He a boss who appears to only focus on your flaws and is looking for ways to make your life miserable? Is He an ignoring husband who abandons you in time of need? Or is He a loving Father? All three of these

---

[17] Aquinas. *Summa Theologica* I-I, Q. 16, art. 1. Accessed at: https://www.newadvent.org/summa/1016.htm . See also Paul Glenn, A Tour of the Summa accessed at: http://www.catholictheology.info/summa-theologica/summa-part1.php?q=34 .

analogies pertaining to their circumstances can be true, but in and of Himself, who God is, is ALWAYS A LOVING FATHER!

This instance of God being a Loving Father for us is found even in the analogous scenarios of life when God seems to be the boss who is a jerk who is always asking things of us but seems to never want to do what we ask of Him and so we tune Him out; or a husband who abandons us whenever we need something, so we grumble against Him. We see this first point of view from Abraham when God asked him to leave his land to go to an unknown place, then to make a covenant with him through circumcision, then to promise him a child which he had to wait for 25 years (see Gen. 12:4; 21:5). We see this point of view from Moses who was called out of slavery to stand up to Pharaoh, take Israel across the Red Sea, then feed and travel with the Israelites and was never able to see the Promised Land (Deut. 32:50-52).

We see the second point of view of grumbling[18] from the Israelites throughout the Old Testament upset with God asking Him for food, water and to go back to Egypt:

"'[The Lord] has heard your grumbling against him. Who are we, that you should grumble against us?' Moses also

---

[18] Ralph Wilson. *Moses: The Reluctant Leader- Section 4: Grumbling, Conflict, and Delegation* (Exodus 15-18). Accessed at: http://www.jesuswalk.com/moses/4_grumbling.htm .

said, 'You will know that it was the LORD when he gives you meat to eat in the evening and all the bread you want in the morning, because he has heard your grumbling against him. Who are we? You are not grumbling against us, but against the LORD'" (Exodus 16:7b-8).

People complaining to the leader about their conditions are really complaining about God's provision for them! Samuel faced the same problem when the people clamored for a king to be over them. "When they said, 'Give us a king to lead us,' this displeased Samuel; so, he prayed to the LORD. And the LORD told him: 'Listen to all that the people are saying to you; it is **not you they have rejected**, but they have **rejected me** as their king. As they have done from the day, I brought them up out of Egypt until this day, forsaking me and serving other gods, so they are doing to you'" (1 Samuel 8:6-8).

I point this out to show that the people of God also fall into these points of view, but let's go a little deeper. How are the people of God's eyes opened? How are their hearts made new? A brief passage with Abram answers this question:

Sometime afterward, the word of the Lord came to Abram in a vision: Do not fear, Abram! I am your shield; I will make your reward very great. But Abram said, "LORD God, what can you give me, if I die childless and have only a servant of my household, Eliezer of Damascus?" Abram continued, "Look, you have given me no offspring, so a servant of my household will be my heir." Then the word of the LORD came to him: No, that one will not be your heir; your own offspring will be your heir. He took him outside and said: Look up at the sky and count the stars, if you can. Just so, he added, will your descendants be. Abram put his faith in the LORD, who attributed it to him as an act of righteousness (Gen. 15:1-6).

Abram approached God with the tough questions (Part 1 of the prescription) and the Lord gave him an answer that was unexpected, and he did not necessarily want to hear. The Lord told Abram to count the stars in the sky and this would be like his descendants! This in and of itself would be an amazing feat as there are hundreds of thousands of stars. But here is what we miss. Often when we read this passage, we think of it as nighttime, but when God asked Abraham to count the stars it was actually daytime as it tells us after a passage of time "when the sun had set and it was dark, there appeared a smoking brazier and flaming torch" (see Gen. 15: 17). You cannot see stars in the day so to count them, Abram would have had to use faith. He would have had to "walk by faith, not by sight" (2Cor. 5:7). This meant trusting God as a Father so He could hear what He was honestly saying to Him and receive His blessing even though it was not visible at the time. Faith united to love yields trust and trust allows you to receive, see, and experience the Father's love which deepens Faith!!

Applying this to our analogies or "real-life examples," when circumstances make God appear like a boss who just wants his way, we must trust God and His love for us and then we can hear a different message. We can realize that often in life God is just inserting a comma, not a period! So, in the first example, the Boss's TRUE and complete reply would sound like, "No, … I want to give you a new title first, then I'll give you the raise too! When can you start?" The boss appeared to be a jerk, but only said "no" so you could become a better employee. Through this, you learned perseverance, and this pays off to him. Scripture tells us this:

> Consider it all joy, my brothers, when you encounter various trials, for you know that the testing of your faith produces perseverance. And let perseverance be perfect, so that you may be perfect and complete, lacking in nothing (Jas. 1:2-4).

We see the boss, i.e., God is actually looking out for you even though He allows you to go through suffering and pain.

In the second instance in which your husband seemed to ignore your phone calls, he actually was not ignoring the phone calls, but was lining things up to keep you safe until he got there once the neighbor informed him about your situation. This brings up the importance of neighbors looking out for one another and letting husbands or family know about things they may be missing when it comes to women who have miscarried or had a stillbirth. Now getting back to the analogy, the husband called a car-assistance agency while he was driving down, had the phone company use the GPS in your phone to find out your location, as well as called a friend who lives near the place you were stranded to go and keep you company until he got there. It seemed like he was ignoring your calls, like he abandoned you in your time of need, but in actuality, he was actively helping. God does this same thing. It may seem like He's distant, like He's focused on everything/everyone but you in your time of grief, but the TRUTH is He continually keeps us as "the apple of His eye" (Deut. 32:10) and promises "I will not leave you as orphans, I will come to you" (Jn. 14:18).

You see the TRUTH is God is a loving boss who no longer calls us servants but friends (Jn. 15:15). God is the good husband of our souls who wants us to know Him intimately by getting to the heart of His name. Remember Isaiah 54:5 from the previous chapter.

Two of the names that God gives for Himself are Rock and Immanuel. The Psalms tell us God is, "Lord, my rock, my fortress, my deliverer, My God, my rock of refuge, my shield, my saving horn, my stronghold" (Ps. 18:3)! Like a good husband he becomes a foundation of strength (stronghold), someone that can help to save us (saving horn), someone who can protect the most precious aspects of our being-i.e., our dignity/worth, and deliverer as someone who transforms our hearts from isolation to consolation through love.

He also gives us the name of Immanuel which means God is with us (Matt. 1:23). We are not alone, God is always with us, "in good times and in bad, in sickness and in health. He will unconditionally love us and honor us all the days of our lives." Does this sound familiar? Yes, these are marriage vows! However, we must realize marriage vows reflect how God loves us! The TRUTH is all of these aspects are combined under the name of God-Father and the more we can learn to walk and live as His children, the more we can be healed from the love, peace, and comfort He wishes to give us during times of miscarriage and stillbirth. Like Abram looking up at the stars during the daytime, we too must trust in God as a heavenly Father whose Word transforms our hearts, deepens our faith, and brings us a peace the world cannot give. This is the reason the Father's living Word gives us hope by saying, "Peace I leave with you; my peace I give to you. Not as the world gives do I give it to you. Do not let your hearts be troubled or afraid. I have told you this so that you might have peace in me. In the world you will have trouble, but take courage, I have conquered the world" (Jn. 14:27; 16: 33). This is the TRUTH: God is Father always, loves us passionately, and wants to be with us always, especially our time of need, especially during and after miscarriage and stillbirth.

Know you and your family's dignity and worth

Now that we have a TRUE picture of God, we can get a true picture of ourselves, our baby who has passed away, and the rest of our family. It is as Vatican II said, "When the creator is forgotten, the creature itself becomes unintelligible."[19] In other words: How we define ourselves depends on how we define God and how we define God is based on how we define ourselves. In coming to the Truth about God, i.e., that He is Father, we can see that we nor our situation, are unintelligible. We are children of God and nothing can ever take that away! Thus, even if we have a miscarriage, we are still loved infinitely by God! That baby is loved infinitely by God! Our family is loved infinitely by God. We are not irreparable or permanently broken but are transformed by the love of God in our relationship to Him as our Father and Redeemer. He sends His spirit upon us, and we can be healed as it dwells within:

---

[19] Vatican II. *Gaudium et Spes: Pastoral Constitution on the Church in the Modern World.* (Citta del Vaticano: Libreria Editrice, Dec. 7, 1965), sec. 36. Accessed at: https://www.vatican.va/archive/hist_councils/ii_vatican_council/documents/vat-ii_const_19651207_gaudium-et-spes_en.html.

The spirit of the Lord God is upon me,
  because the LORD has anointed me;
He has sent me to bring good news to the afflicted,
  to bind up the brokenhearted...
To comfort all who mourn;
  to place on those who mourn in Zion
  a diadem instead of ashes,
To give them oil of gladness instead of mourning,
  a glorious mantle instead of a faint spirit (Is. 61:1-3).

Our dignity and worth as individuals and family are beyond price. Our value is greater than a diadem, not low as ashes. We are called to live in the oil of gladness instead of mourning and to hold a glorious mantle rather than a faint spirit! In God's Spirit, we can become a new creation; a new way of living out a love that goes beyond the grave for:

What can separate us from the love of Christ? Will anguish, or distress, or persecution, or famine, or nakedness, or peril, or the sword? No, in all these things we conquer overwhelmingly through him who loved us. For I am convinced that neither death, nor life, nor angels, nor principalities, nor present things, nor future things, nor powers, nor height, nor depth, nor any other creature will be able to separate us from the love of God in Christ Jesus our Lord (Rom. 8: 35, 37-39).

We conquer overwhelmingly through the God who has loved us. This conquering means maintaining our identity and worth, especially in our families. As all are renewed in Christ and made a new creation which nobody or nothing, not even death, can take away!

Help: Accompaniment vs Abandonment

The pastoral perspective must be improved as sadly, there is not always pastoral help in situations involving miscarriage and stillbirth. There are numerous mothers who have had experiences talking to clergy who do not know what to do or where to send them for help. One Catholic woman who had a miscarriage was in the hospital and a Protestant pastor came to visit the room. He asked her if she would like a "prayer service". The woman responded, "No thank you, that's generous, but my Church will do something for me." She came to find out later when she went back to her parish, her parish priest told her there really is not much he could do for her. Another woman was told by another clergyman that he wouldn't do anything for the family because he was sure the baby was not in hell. Then a third woman said the priest simply said, "I'm sorry, but what do you want me to do about it." Sadly, many priests unknowingly and non-maliciously manifest a perspective leaving families feeling abandoned. Julie Collazo explains in an article interviewing many women about their experiences with miscarriage in the Church:

> In fact, when she and other members of the parish's Respect Life committee wanted to address prenatal diagnoses, which frequently prevent a woman from carrying a child to term, as a "life issue," their priest responded by saying, "What is that?"
>
> For Katherine, the question stung. But it wasn't entirely surprising; miscarriage and pregnancy losses, as common as they are, remain one of the most neglected aspects of ministry within the church. Families affected by pregnancy loss are reaching out for support from their parishes and clergy, but too often they feel as if they are reaching into a void. Few priests are equipped to deal with this sensitive and painful topic, and most of the resources that do exist within the church focus on pro-life issues—not always the most helpful pastoral response to a family in mourning. While independent ministries are rising up to fulfill this unmet need, a more concentrated response is needed among priests, chaplains, and pastoral caregivers.[20]

---

[20] Julie Collazo. *U.S Catholic*. "The quiet grief of miscarriage: The Church Needs a Better Pastoral Response Toward Women and Families Who Experience Miscarriage and Stillbirth." Nov.

This has to change! It is as the book of James tells us:

> What good is it, my brothers, if someone says he has faith but does not have works? Can that faith save him? If a brother or sister has nothing to wear and has no food for the day, and one of you says to them, "Go in peace, keep warm, and eat well," but you do not give them the necessities of the body, what good is it? So also, faith of itself, if it does not have works, is dead (James 2: 14-17).

Our Faith tells us that this miscarried baby is a precious gift from God and should be honored as such, but how do we do "the work" of carrying this out practically? How can we show honor to the baby who was lost, the parents who have lost a child, and to a community that is grieving the loss of one of their members? This is the reason we must shift from an apparent *Abandonment Model* to an *Accompaniment Model.* Please note, I think many clergy have good intentions; they just do not know how to deal with this issue. Thus, we need to do a better job of changing from a model in which families are painfully asking, "Where is the Church and God?" to a model that demonstrates in a loving way, "God is now here and is accompanying you-the Immanuel Model."

2016 Edition. Accessed at: http://www.uscatholic.org/articles/201610/quiet-grief-miscarriage-30794 .

Information -Canon Law, Order of Christian Funerals, and Catechism of the Catholic Church

Pastorally Addressing Anger

There is a lot of heartache, harsh feelings, and even anger because of what people simply do not know. Let us start with two topics concerning anger: a life taken and accepting God's will since we are Christians who strive to live as His disciples. Sometimes, families get angry because they can't believe that God "took their child." Do we just have to pretend "we're not angry" in order to be "good Christians?" Other times, families get angry because they think the Church, particularly their clergy, simply do not care about their miscarriage or stillbirth. Both are not true!

Anger results when there is a perceived injustice towards someone or something whom we love. [21] From this, we can address questions concerning anger. First, we must realize that anger is a natural emotion and is not something we should just try to snuff out so we can be "good Christians." That is not Christianity, but stoicism! The big difference between Stoic anger and Christian anger is that Christian anger is tied to justice and hope. St. Augustine states this beautifully when he said, "Hope has two beautiful daughters; their

---

[21] Aquinas. *Summa Theologica* II-I, Q. 46, art. 7. Accessed at: https://www.newadvent.org/summa/2046.htm#article1.

names are anger and courage: Anger at the way things are, and Courage to see that they do not remain as they are."

Our emotions are data points and if the emotion of anger comes up, we must look at the roots of the perceived injustice. We can then determine how to serenely change things, so they do not remain the same. I write serenely because this change must involve true serenity which is stated in the Serenity Prayer, "Lord, grant me the serenity to accept the things I cannot change, courage to change the things I can, and wisdom to know the difference. Amen."

The perceived injustice comes from the fact that we had a child, but it seems to have been "taken from us." These are valid emotions, but the reality is a child is not a right owed to us in justice, but a gift given to us in love. Thus, as a clergyman once said, "We must not make our question, 'Why did you take my child' but 'Why did you give me the blessing of time with my child in the first place?'" If we can focus on the "blessing of time aspect, we realize we should not hate God because He has chosen to bring His gift back to Himself earlier than we would have liked.

Secondly, you may feel anger because it seems that God has taken your parenthood away. But this is not true. You are still parents of that child who is now in the merciful embrace of a loving God; it is just now that parenthood is lived out in a different way. It is a spiritual, supernatural motherhood or fatherhood instead of just a natural, earthly way of parenting. This is crucial because spiritual motherhood and fatherhood are often a forgotten part of parenting. Marcel LeJuene, parent and Catholic Missionary emphasizes this, "Your main objective as a parent is to get your kids to heaven. Let this be your constant vision and goal."[22] This must be your goal because this is God's will and the reason, He gave you children in the first place. Scripture tells us this, "This is the will of God, your holiness." (1Thess. 4:3). The Lord does not want you to forget this which is why He gives you visible signs through clergy, religious sisters, and consecrated laity to encourage us. Connecting your children to the Heavenly Father is a true and important part of parenthood and that does not stop at the grave. There is sadness because we are not able to carry out our biological motherhood/fatherhood, but there is not an injustice because you are still parents through your spiritual motherhood/fatherhood. Let us pray for and with your beloved little ones often to live out your parenthood. This connects us to hope with love. This connection transforms your parenthood. Hence, St. Paul would tell us:

> If then you were raised with Christ, seek what is above, where Christ is seated at the right hand of God. Think of

---

[22] Marcel LeJuene. *Catholic Missionary Disciples.* "Catholic Parenting - How To Do Everything You Can To Get Your Kid To Heaven!" Accessed at: https://catholicmissionarydisciples.com/news/catholic-parenting .

what is above, not of what is on earth. For you have died, and your life is hidden with Christ in God. When Christ your life appears, then you too will appear with him in glory (Col. 3:1-4).

If we keep our view on the things above and not simply what is below, we can have hope and trust in our Loving Father's plan. Take courage to live out your parenthood in serenity.

This brings us to the other issue of anger, that is it seems that many clergy do not care about families with miscarriages or stillbirths. In all honesty, this simply is not on the radar of many clergy because they never hear about it in their parish conversations. They also are underprepared for this in their formation and life experience. A priest from Orlando explains:

All of this is not to say that priests don't wish to better acknowledge the needs of women and families who are grieving. But it's difficult when they receive little or no training in seminary. "You learn how to perform a wedding and say Mass when you're a young priest," says Father John McCormick, the rector of St. James Cathedral in Orlando, but when it comes to ministerial responses to miscarriage, "you're left to your own devices."[23]

---

[23] Julie Collazo. *U.S Catholic.* "The quiet grief of miscarriage: The Church Needs a Better Pastoral Response Toward Women

Also, we should remember that most celibate clergy have a limited idea of family life and unless they have siblings who have experienced miscarriage; this is probably never brought up as a topic of discussion. Some clergy must grow in their pastoral experience and knowledge of miscarriage and stillbirth. The clergy do care, but realistically they are underprepared in showing that care to their flock pertaining to the issue of miscarriage.

Pastoral Information

Therefore, we will now give information to clergy about pastoral approaches and offer some recommendations. Many have never had a class on the topic nor are given information on it. We hope that this section helps to enable clergy to carry out the Immanuel Approach Pastoral Model.

The first thing we must remember is that all clergy are deacons. They have an indelible mark of deacon on their souls as a permanent or transitional deacon, a priest, and even as a bishop. So, each Order in the three degrees of Holy Orders is intimately connected to the diaconate. This conforms all clergy to Jesus Christ, the primary deacon who

---

and Families Who Experience Miscarriage and Stillbirth." Nov. 2016 Edition. Accessed at: http://www.uscatholic.org/articles/201610/quiet-grief-miscarriage-30794 .

came "not to be served but to serve" (Mk. 10:45). Thus, the Church Hierarchy is comprised of deacons, deacon-priests, and deacon-bishops. Each Order of deacon must pay special attention to these words from the *National Directory of the Formation, Ministry, and Life of the Permanent Diaconate*:

> "The deacon must strive, therefore, to serve all of humanity ...while devoting particular care to the suffering... Ultimately, the deacon's principle diakonia—a sign of the Church's mission— "should bring [all whom he serves] to an experience of God's love and move [them] to conversion by opening [their] heart[s] to the work of grace."[24]

We must open up the hearts of all to the work of grace and experience God's love. In other words, pastorally move from abandonment to accompaniment. This means knowing what the Church teaches about miscarried/stillborn babies so we can know what can be done for miscarried babies and their families. This will be the last section of this chapter.

---

[24] United States Conference of Catholic Bishops. *National Directory of the Formation, Ministry, and Life of the Permanent Diaconate* (Washington DC: USCCB Publishing, 2005), para. 85.

Making the Church Community Aware While Forming Support

The Church encourages accompaniment through Scripture as well as Tradition in the *Catechism of the Catholic Church*. She also applies these two sources of Revelation to her practical pastoral recommendations in *Canon Law* (the laws that regulate the operations of the Roman Catholic Church), the *Book of Blessings*, and the *Order of Christian Funerals* Rites.

In Scripture, Jesus says, "Let the children come to me; do not prevent them, for the kingdom of God belongs to such as these" (Mk. 10:14). This is the Accompaniment Principle for the child as well as the Lord's mandate to help the parents unite their child to Jesus. Thus, we must accompany the child to the Heavenly Father's love as well as accompany the families with the necessary help they desire. Parents of children who lost their child may ask, "Where can I find help to deepen my faith, love my child, and maintain hope for him or her in the resurrection? Psalm 124: 8 tells us the answer. It says, "Our help is in the name of the LORD, who made heaven and earth." We should receive help from those who carry the name of the LORD, the Church!

Thus, the Church calls her clergy and the laity to help those who have lost a child by laying a foundation of love. This comes through the works of mercy in which we are "merciful like our Heavenly Father" (Lk. 6:36). The book of

Tobit tells us it is "a charitable deed", a corporal work of mercy, to bury the dead (see Tob. 1:16-17). It is also charitable to do spiritual works of mercy: Counseling the doubtful, comforting the sorrowful, praying for the living and the dead, and instructing the ignorant (sharing knowledge). Helping the child to encounter the mercy of God connects the child to embrace the theological virtue of faith which is the basis for the child receiving the application of Baptism even outside of time.

Therefore, *The Code of Canon Law* states, "The local ordinary can permit children whom the parents intended to baptize but who died before baptism to be given ecclesiastical funerals." [25] Canon Law also allows miscarried/stillborn babies to be buried and to have funerals. *The Order of Christian Funerals* and *Catechism of the Catholic Church* even encourage us to do so. *The Order of Christian Funerals* states, "Christians celebrate the funeral rites to offer worship, praise, and thanksgiving to God for the gift of life which has now been returned to God, the author of life…The Church through its funeral rites commends the dead to God's merciful love and pleads for the forgiveness of their sins" [including original sin]. [26] The *Catechism* continues this theme:

---

[25] Code of Canon Law. Can. 1183 §2. Accessed at: http://www.vatican.va/archive/ENG1104/__P4C.HTM

[26] *Order of Christian Funerals*, General Introduction (New Jersey: Catholic Book Publishing, 1998), sec. 5-6.

"Since Christ died for all, and since all men are in fact called to one and the same destiny, which is divine, we must hold that the Holy Spirit offers to all the possibility of being made partakers, in a way known to God, of the Paschal mystery." Every man who is ignorant of the Gospel of Christ and of his Church, but seeks the truth and does the will of God in accordance with his understanding of it, can be saved. It may be supposed that such persons would have desired Baptism explicitly if they had known its necessity. As regards *children who have died without Baptism*, the Church can only entrust them to the mercy of God, as she does in her funeral rites for them. Indeed, the great mercy of God who desires that all men should be saved, and Jesus' tenderness toward children which caused him to say: "Let the children come to me, do not hinder them," allow us to hope that there is a way of salvation for children who have died without Baptism. All the more urgent is the Church's call not to prevent little children coming to Christ through the gift of holy Baptism.[27]

---

[27] Libreria Editrice Vaticana. *Catechism of the Catholic Church, 2nd Ed.* (Citta del Vaticana: Libreria Editrice Vaticana, 1997), nn. 1260-1261.

Consequently, since the Faith of the Church is the faith provided for Baptism and to obtain its effects; if that consent is
given, the Child can have an ecclesiastical funeral (Can.
1183.2). The unbaptized child can have a funeral by the
Church just as catechumens can receive Christian burial
even if they die before they come into the Church.[28] St. Ber-
nard of Clairvaux, 12th Century Doctor of the Church and
one of the most revered men on earth at that time, summarizes all of this beautifully with the words he wrote in a letter
to a family who suffered a miscarriage:

> *In response to their question, "What is going to happen to*
> *my child? The child didn't get baptized," St. Bernard said,*
> "Your faith spoke for this child. Baptism for this child
> was only delayed by time. Your faith suffices. The waters
> of your womb — were they not the waters of life for this
> child? Look at your tears. Are they not like the waters of
> baptism? Do not fear this. God's ability to love is greater
> than our fears. Surrender everything to God."[29]

---

[28] See *Order of Christian Funerals* #18 as well as Canon 1183 in
the *Code of Canon Law.*

[29] Catholic Miscarriage Support. Quotes on Suffering. Accessed   at: https://www.catholicmiscarriagesupport.com/emo-
tional/quotes-on-suffering/

So, the *Order of Christian Funerals* encourages the clergy to offer up funeral rites in order to accompany the family in the ministry of consolation. This lines up with the three-spiritual works of mercy consisting of counseling the doubtful, comforting the sorrowful, and praying for the living and the dead. It notes:

> The celebration of the Christian funeral brings hope and consolation to the living. While proclaiming the Gospel of Jesus Christ and witnessing to Christian hope in the resurrection, the funeral rites also recall to all who take part in them God's mercy and judgment and meet the human need to turn always to God in times of crisis…The Church calls each member of Christ's Body-priest, deacon, layperson — to participate in the ministry of consolation: to care for the dying, to pray for the dead, to comfort those who mourn."[30]

Since there are technically three funeral rites offered to the dead: A Vigil-sometimes known as the Viewing, The Funeral liturgy, and the Committal (see *Order of Christian Funerals*#11), as well as a blessing which the Church offers for those whom have had a miscarriage, we should imitate the heart of Christ for whom, "there is no distinction between

---

[30] Catholic Book Publishing. *Order of Christian Funerals* (New Jersey: Catholic Book Publishing Co., 1998), sec. 7-8.

Jew and Greek; the same Lord *is Lord of all and is generous to all who call on him.*" (Rom. 10:12) [emphasis mine]. This means being generous in offering at the Service all the rites and blessings the Church offers to the couple who are in mourning.

It may be impractical to offer a Vigil service being that the couple may only be able to meet for one burial ceremony. Thus, the two Rites of the Rite of Committal with Final Commendation for Children[31] beginning with the Ecclesial blessing for parents who miscarried [32]can be administered in the Rites for parents who would have had their miscarried/stillborn child baptized but were unable if they want all the ecclesiastical funeral rites prescribed to their child in Can. 1183.2. Thus, the parents receive a blessing from the Church as well as the child receives an ecclesiastical funeral at this meeting. This is a blessing and can bring closure to many families letting them know the Church is with them in honoring the life and death of their precious child.

Church Awareness and Support

---

[31] Catholic Book Publishing. *Order of Christian Funerals* (New Jersey: Catholic Book Publishing Co., 1998), sec.327-336.

[32] Catholic Book Publishing. *Book of Blessings* (New York: Catholic Book Publishing Co., 1989), sec. 279-294.

Now that you can share with clergy information about what they can canonically do to honor your child and family with the funeral rites of the church as well as help them understand they CAN bury your child and even are encouraged to do so by *Canon Law*, the *Catechism*, and the Church's Funeral Rites; we can get to the last letter of the Spiritual Prescription. This is the letter "M" which stands for "Making the Church Community aware and forming support."

We must make clergy aware that miscarriage and stillbirth is an issue in their parishes because as noted earlier, this is not on most of their radar. We must remember most priest only get to "talk" with their parishioners for a moment before or after Mass and the topic of miscarriage usually does not come up while you are shaking hands or saying goodbye after Mass. The only other time many priests get to talk to their parishioners is in the Confessional. The priests may hear about "anger towards God" about losing their child in Confession, but because it's under the seal, the priest is not allowed to mention nor act on it. ***The majority of priests however do not even really know that this is a problem in their parishes. And those that do know about it, do not know how to pastorally care for their families.*** If you never hear about something, you will assume that there is nothing wrong and this is where many priests are pertaining to the topic of miscarriage. Many deacons however, especially those who are married do know about miscarriage as they have most likely experienced one within their families.

Deacons generally do have this on their radar but are not very vocal about it because they know the pain that occurred in the loss of their own child or family member. Advocating for more of an awareness can open a wound that may not have healed amidst his own family. Deacons can make priests more aware of this issue in their parishes.

It is crucial for parishioner to talk about miscarriage more with clergy and for clergy to talk more with their flock about miscarriage. Clergy that are aware of this issue need to help more clergy to become aware of it. Deacons can talk to the parochial vicars and pastors about this topic and then as clergy in the parish make a plan to address the topic possibly in homilies, marriage preparation, and pastoral accompaniment. Clergy should make more time to talk and be present with their parishioners, so they feel comfortable talking to them about such heart-breaking issues in a calm and non-rushed manner. Just being there to listen is a huge step in helping families to heal from the loss of a child.

Here are five other ways clergy can raise miscarriage and stillbirth awareness involving liturgy and sacramentals:

1. Mention families who have lost a baby at the General Intercessions at Mass
2. Homilies
3. Wedding Preparation
4. Vespers (Evening Prayer)

5. Do a Rite of Blessing for Parents Who Have Suffered Miscarriage during the Month of Child-Loss Awareness.

Clergy can mention the families who have lost children in the General Intercessions at Mass. Another thing clergy can do, as stated above, is to mention miscarriage in homilies every now and then as it is a relevant topic in the lives of the parishioners. Every day someone in the parish has had a miscarriage or knows someone impacted by a miscarriage but it might be brought up once a year. It would be nice to speak about it to give hope to parishioners as well as help lift the "taboo" of child-loss amidst topics in the Church.

A third action that clergy can take is to mention some statistics of child loss in their wedding preparations. If one in four pregnancies end in child loss, then, it should be mentioned in wedding preparation and Engagement Encounter Weekends as it is likely that about 25% of the couples attending will experience a miscarriage/stillbirth during their marriage. As a Church, we should help people prepare for marriage and one of the neglected preparations is the possibility of the miscarriage or stillbirth. It is important to mention this because when it happens to a family; they usually are in shock because they never thought it could happen to them and in their minds, it is not a common problem. Because of this, many families think that "God is singling them out" and it causes them to be angry with God. If we can prepare couples to understand this is a possibility, it can prevent some of the potential future anger, shock, and angst for the couple.

A fourth thing that could be done is including the list of families who have lost a child or a child whose funeral you have done in Vespers (Evening Prayer) once a month since the last petition in Evening Prayer involves the souls of the departed.

A fifth item is during National Child-Loss Awareness month (October), clergy can do the *Rite of Blessing for Parents Who have Suffered a Miscarriage* [33]for their parish after Mass along with a Rosary or Chaplet of Our Lady of Sorrows since October is also the month of the Rosary. I know that I have done this (a homily and given this blessing) as a deacon and there were so many families that were appreciative of it as "they could finally talk about it with someone."

This brings us to things that the Church community as the Mystical Body of Christ can do to support families. Since the loss of the child is still taboo in the Church, a meeting of families who have gone through this could be a tremendous asset to a parish or Church community. Many families are looking for resources of support but have no idea of where to begin. I also think parish pro-life groups should make this a topic in their agenda. This is a pro-life issue of being able

---

[33] Catholic Book Publishing. *Book of Blessings* (New York: Catholic Book Publishing Co., 1989), sec. 279-294.

to support and honor the life of the baby in the womb. The funerals are great witnesses to the dignity and sanctity of life. Parishioners could also choose to accompany a family in prayer as prayer links us together in God's love and connects us to the Church. It can bring great comfort to a family knowing that another family is praying for them and has made their little one part of their family as well. Another thing we can do is encourage families to include their deceased sons/daughters and brothers/sisters in some of their family prayers. This could be a particular Family-Rosary dedicated to the lost family member in October (National Child-Loss Awareness month) or November (the month of the Holy Souls) or a Chaplet of Divine Mercy continually entrusting the child and family to the Mercy of God.

In conclusion, we see that the Spiritual Prescription is an in-depth prescription that can help us to find a way to move forward by remembering the phrase "**ASK HIM**." We must **A**pproach God and ask Him those tough questions that are in our hearts. Then we should **S**ee God in truth. This allows us to know that God is not a bad boss looking to punish us, shut us down, or an inattentive husband who doesn't care when we are in need. Instead, He is a loving Father who always wants to be with us and even wants to walk with us amidst the pain of losing a child. This brings us to **K**nowing our dignity. We are not irreparable or permanently broken but loved by God along with our child and so have infinite worth. Once we start to **ASK**, then we can continue to get

Help. We are able to live out and encourage our clergy to adapt a pastoral approach of accompaniment instead of seeming abandonment. To do this we have to share and learn Information. This information helps to understand that our child can have funeral rites and Scripture, the *Catechism*, and the Church's *Canon Law* and Liturgical books encourage us to do so. It also links our minds to a knowledge of hope that our child is entrusted to the mercy of God and that God can do marvelous things for our little one once we entrust him or her to God's love. That brought us to Making the Church Community aware and forming support systems. We offered many ideas for clergy to do, as well as activities the parish community and family could do to support the loss of a child. We see that God supplies many answers to questions we may have through child-loss which is why it is fitting that the Spiritual Prescription for peace and healing is a simple reminder to **ASK HIM!**

Prescription 5

Intersecting Family Perspectives
(Family Response to Grief)

**"For this reason, I kneel before the Father, from whom
every family in heaven and on earth is named, that he
may grant you in accord with the riches of his glory to be
strengthened with power through his Spirit in the inner
self, and that Christ may dwell in your hearts through
faith; that you, rooted and grounded in love"**

(Eph. 3:14-17).

Note: In this Chapter, the Doctor's perspective is italicized
for a calming "medical" effect while reading.

Deacon Perspective:

The family is a place of love and healing. As the *Catechism of the Catholic Church* notes, "The home is the first
school of Christian life and 'a school for human enrichment.'
Here one learns endurance and the joy of work, fraternal
love, generous — even repeated — forgiveness, and above all
divine worship in prayer and the offering of one's life" (*CCC*,
1657). The family is a place of enrichment in which we grow
in our ability to love, sacrifice, forgive, and offer one's life as

a gift to God through our vocations. The offering of one's life, especially when one loses someone he or she loves, is crucial in the healing process. The family is the place that helps us to sift through our grief, depression, anger, and grow in love. The family gets through the journey together, but the journey of each member of the family will look different. A mom's and wife's grief will look different from a dad and husband's grief. Both parents' grief will look different from the sibling's grief depending on age, sex, and temperament. Therefore, we as the deacon and the doctor will go back and forth in this prescription looking at the various perspectives for the family as well as for each of the members of the family in general.

Doctor Perspective:

While I would love to share Deacon's perspective on the family being a place of love and healing, we should also be aware that's not always the case for everyone. Often there may be toxic dysfunction present in the family system that greatly exacerbates the pain of child loss. We hope to offer both, at times, intersecting perspectives on family, society, and friend responses to grief. We agree that addressing the family environment is critical to processing child loss. Either way, we are part of family systems and need to work within those systems; sometimes they can be a source of wonderful support, and other times, we need to learn how to establish boundaries to protect our mental health when family members' behaviors are contributing to mental health issues.

Deacon Perspective:

To start off, we will look at the family in general and how it deals with grief and depression. Pope John Paul II notes that there are "different, complex aspects of depression: they range from chronic sickness, more or less permanent, to a fleeting state linked to difficult events - conjugal and family conflicts, serious work problems, states of loneliness... - that involve a crack, or even fracture in social, professional or family relationships. This disease is often accompanied by an existential and spiritual crisis that leads to an inability to perceive the meaning of life."[34] Grief can lead to depression and depression can lead to the inability to perceive the meaning of life. Thus, losing a child can have a literal life-changing existential effect on a family, particularly with their faith and connection to one another and the community.

---

[34] Pope John Paul II. *Address of John Paul II: To the Participants in the 18th International Conference Promoted by the Pontifical Council for Health Pastoral Care on the Theme of "Depression"*, sec. 2. Friday, 14 November, 2003. Accessed at: https://www.vatican.va/content/john-paul-ii/en/speeches/2003/november/documents/hf_jp-ii_spe_20031114_pc-hlthwork.html

The faith perspective with grief and depression is often left out, but it is an important perspective in healing. Many families go to psychologists and counseling (and rightly so) to help them grieve. But many people don't address the spiritual aspect of grief as St. John Paul notes, "Depression is always a spiritual trial."[35] It is a trial that must be addressed in a way that includes the spiritual plane because if not, there can be serious harm done to faith or even the loss of faith altogether. But if God is the "name from whom every family in heaven and earth takes its name" (Eph. 3:14-15); a family cannot restore its name after the loss of a child, i.e., a trial without Him.

This is the reason John Paul II encourages those who are not looking after the individual or family therapeutically to help them in their spiritual journey. Again, he writes, "The role of those who care for depressed persons … consists above all in helping them to rediscover their self-esteem, confidence in their own abilities, interest in the future, the desire to live."[36] Therefore, we will look at how to help a family rediscover self-esteem, confidence in their abilities, interest in the future, and give them a desire to live.

First, we will look at rediscovering self-esteem. In order to rediscover self-esteem, we must first look at what makes up our self. This is the Intimacy challenge because intimacy

---

[35] Ibid., sec. 3.

[36] Ibid.

at its heart is our desire that our minds, bodies, and souls say, "In-to-me-see." This means self-reflection, but also a communal connection because we are all made for love which connects people heart to heart. There are six types of intimacy which make up the "self". These are:

1. Physical
2. Emotional
3. Intellectual
4. Recreational
5. Spiritual
6. Social

Each of these types of intimacy must be addressed, nourished, and healed. Let us define these and then we can apply them to the family as a whole, and to the individual members of the family.

Physical Intimacy: Touch is a very important factor in any relationship. We need a loving touch. Touch communicates love, kindness and acceptance. Touch can help create closeness in marriage [and a family]. Physical intimacy is basically about being passionate with each other, which can range from anywhere between hugging to cuddling on the couch. It also means being connected with your partner [and your family].[37]

Doctor Perspective

After a miscarriage or stillbirth, physical intimacy is often the last thing on a woman's mind. In many cases, the idea of physical intimacy is distressing because you may have anxiety about getting pregnant again and losing another baby. For others, they rush into physical intimacy in the hope of getting pregnant again quickly but perhaps are not ready for the emotional consequences of not processing the trauma. The physical and lasting pain after a miscarriage may last weeks or even months making physical intimacy incredibly difficult. However, as Deacon points out, physical intimacy can be as simple as a hug. I would caution husbands and wives who have suffered a miscarriage to take things very slowly with physical intimacy and be on the same page as far as what they are comfortable with

---

[37] Rachel Pace. *6 Forms of Intimacy to Build a Strong Marriage: Incorporate These Types of Intimacy into Your Relationship and Watch Your Marriage Thrive.* Accessed at: https://www.beliefnet.com/love-family/relationships/marriage/6-forms-of-intimacy-to-build-a-strong-marriage.aspx . The definitions provided in all the types of intimacy except for Social intimacy come from this article.

and what it looks like post loss. It may take time to reconnect physically after the loss of a child, and it may look completely different. A mother who had a second trimester miscarriage shares:

> *"I couldn't even hold my husband's hand after my miscarriage or be hugged by friends or family. Just being touched would trigger me. I was in so much physical and emotional pain after being poked and prodded by doctors at the hospitals that I just wanted to be left alone. For weeks after I would recoil when my other children would try to hug me. Months later when I was ready to try to conceive again, I remember breaking down in tears when my husband tried to give me a kiss. I came to realize later that even though I desperately wanted to try for another child, I was terrified to get pregnant and then lose another baby. It was a very slow process for us to get back to a sense of normalcy in our marriage."*

Physical intimacy is different for every couple. It's a beautiful and healthy way to express your love for one another. Following a miscarriage or stillbirth, go as slow as you need to when rebuilding what it means to be physically intimate. Your body has endured an unimaginable shock. It may take time before you are ready to be intimate in the same way as before the loss, but it is important to take steps forward however that may look for you now, i.e., a hug, holding hands, a kiss on the cheek, etc. Try not to pressure yourself to meet a certain timeline. Listen to your body, you will know when you are ready! Another important thing rarely discussed after a miscarriage or still birth, is the long-term impact on the relationship. A recent study found "couples who had experienced a miscarriage had a 22 percent greater risk of divorcing or ending their relationship than couples who had not lost a baby. For couples who had suffered a stillbirth, the risk was 40 percent higher." [38] *It is important to not overlook the psychological impact on a relationship/marriage. I always recommend attending couples therapy after suffering a miscarriage or stillbirth to have a safe place to process your feelings together.*

Deacon Note:

Emotional Intimacy: Emotional intimacy, which is all about sharing feelings and desires, is another type of intimacy. It is about being yourself with your family and sharing about your loss.

---

[38] Robert Wood Johnson Foundation. *Miscarriage or Stillbirth Increases Risk of Breakup or Divorce.* Accessed at: https://www.rwjf.org/en/library/articles-and-news/2010/11/miscarriage-or-stillbirth-increases-risk-of-breakup-or-divorce.html

Doctor Perspective: Absolutely agree with Deacon Anthony! Being able to share and process your feelings openly with family is healthy and helps as you navigate the trauma of the loss. If your family does not do well with emotional processing, this might be a good time to normalize this as a new concept for them. As a parent, it's a wonderful lesson to teach our children the value of processing both positive and negative emotions. If you come from an extended family that did not value discussing their feelings, this is a great time to set new boundaries. Always self-advocate. You can say this is what you and your husband need right now, and they can help and engage with you or they can stay out of it! I know it's hard but try not to feel guilty when you are advocating, even with well-meaning family members.

Deacon Note

Intellectual Intimacy: Intellectual intimacy is about being on the same page. You have a mutual understanding of the things that you find important as people. As a couple or family, you make it a priority to grow in knowledge about a certain topic like cooking, history, art, or even family events. You choose to connect through knowledge about a specific topic together.

Doctor Perspective: Learning new things together as a couple or family is a very healthy way to build bridges. Learning new skills and gaining knowledge together is fun and helps keep your mind active. It also helps unite the family with a common objective. As a couple or family, you could make a list of things you want to learn and then make a schedule for how to meet your goals.

Deacon Note

> **Recreational Intimacy:** Taking Time Out For Each Other. It's all about being active together and doing things together that you [as a family] enjoy.

Doctor Perspective

Yes! Stop and take some time as a family to do things that are leisure based. Perhaps not immediately after the loss, but when you are ready, try not to delay engaging in innovative recreational activities. It may give you a great serotonin boost that you need! As a note, a few weeks after my miscarriage my husband and I went to a painting class. He's not into painting, and I can barely draw a stick figure, but it was something different and unusual, and helped shift our environmental perspective for a few hours. It was actually a therapeutic experience. Again, when you are ready!

Deacon Note

> **Spiritual Intimacy:** This kind of intimacy is about shared religious beliefs and religious practices.

Doctor Perspective

It can be helpful when couples/families share similar religious/spiritual beliefs, especially about death. However, that's not always the case. For example, while my husband converted to Catholicism when we got married, his family is not Catholic. Also, different cultural traditions impact beliefs and practices. My family is of Colombian descent, his family is fourth generation American. Our cultures view death in very different ways. It would be helpful if as a couple/family you could discuss your views about death and the afterlife and come to a place of mutual understanding and respect, even if the views are different.

Deacon Note

> **Social Intimacy:** This is doing things as a couple/family in society. This involves connecting with other families and neighbors, volunteering as a family to help others, as well as supporting other couples/families as a group. As recreational intimacy is geared towards "recreating" the intimacy within the couple/family/or group, social

intimacy is geared towards connecting with others outwardly as a couple/family/or group.

Dr. Rickey Miller, back in the late 1970's, proposed the idea that close relationships play a protective role in moderating the effects of stress. This idea was quite novel. He wrote, "I hypothesize that people who have relationships that are closer and more supportive can cope better with stress and are healthier. I developed and validated a measure of social intimacy, The Miller Social Intimacy Scale (MSIS). My research showed that people who have low levels of social intimacy are prone to higher levels of emotional disturbance especially when they experience many negative life changing events or few positive ones. People who have higher levels of social intimacy cope better. The data have been consistent in pointing out the importance that close relationships have on our health and ability to cope with stress.[39]

Doctor Perspective

Social support from friends and your community is critical after the death of a loved one. Sometimes when you don't have

---

[39] Dr. Rickey Miller, Psychologist. Social Intimacy. Accessed at: https://rickeymillerpsychologist.com/research .

a close relationship with your extended family, the support of
friends can be extremely comforting.

Deacon Note

In looking to apply these types of intimacy to make the person and family whole again and reclaim their family name, we must apply them to life. There are some families I've worked with after the loss of the child who lose physical intimacy. The couple stops touching one another, even holding hands, kissing, and having sexual intimacy because "they are afraid of what might happen." They also stop hugging their other children because it "hurts too bad." Emotionally and intellectually, walls come up and families stop sharing their day with one another because a husband may want to "just move on" while the wife is still trying to process the loss. This leads to families not spending time with one another and just enjoying one another (Recreational Intimacy) and disconnecting from their communities (Social intimacy). All of this leads to disconnecting from God and the Church because all the other aspects of life are leading to isolation which we have already discussed earlier results in an unhealthy place in life.

So, we must look at what we can do to strengthen these six types of intimacy for the family and the individual. The family must connect physically. This means extending the great gift of touch. Touch is crucial for human development.

Jonathan Jones interviewed Dr. Tiffany Field, head of the Touch Research Institute at the University of Miami's Miller School of Medicine and explains the value of touch. He writes, "From the time we are in the womb through our elderly years, touch plays a primary role in our development and physical and mental well-being. Innovative studies on touch continue to show the importance of physical contact in early development, communication, personal relationships, and fighting disease." [40] Losing a child or a sibling is extremely hard both on the heart and on the body! But the body can help heal the heart which is why physical intimacy, i.e., touch, is so important. Dr. Field notes that kids who are hugged more are "less aggressive, both verbally and physically." [41] This can be crucial when the children are angry and throwing their toys and/or food (yes, I've experienced both of these at the same time along with tears with my nieces and nephews) because they are having problems dealing with the loss of their sibling. Touch also helps to deal with stress. A good hug or a massage between couples can activate pressure

---

[40] Jonathan Jones. Greater Good Magazine. *Why Physical Touch Matters for Your Well-Being: Physical contact seems to be declining in modern life. But what happens when we lack human touch?* November 16, 2018. Accessed at: https://greatergood.berkeley.edu/article/item/why_physical_touch_matters_for_your_well_being

[41] Ibid.

receptors and make us less tense and less-depressed. As Dr. Field shares:

> What happens is you're stimulating pressure receptors, and vagal activity increases. Vagus is one of the 12 cranial nerves, and it has a lot of branches all over the body from the gastrointestinal system and the heart to our vocal cords and so forth. We have measured vagal activity and that increases, and with that, you get a decrease in cortisol, the stress hormone. There's an increase in serotonin, which is the body's natural antidepressant and anti-pain chemical. You get a decrease in Substance P, that senses pain.[42]

So, a great hug during times of duress cannot only decrease stress hormones, unleash much needed antidepressants and anti-pain chemicals like serotonin, but can also help you with your digestion so you can enjoy all the food that people are hopefully bringing over so you can have time to grieve. Touch and physical intimacy can also help with your everyday performances at work or throughout the day. If there is a big project coming up at work, or the kids have a stressful test coming up, or if you're a stay-at-home parent; a hug can make the day a little brighter so you can feel calm and perform better. Dr. Tiffany Field once again notes,

---

[42] Ibid.

"[there are] some studies showing that if you get hugged by your partner before a stressful condition like giving a speech or doing math problems, people do better. Performance is better if they've been hugged by a partner before the stress."[43] Thus, we need to have physical intimacy to help the family as a whole deal with loss.

The body helps to relieve the stress of the emotions and heal the heart so that you can continue to live life even after the loss of your child. While you are hugging one another, you can also check on each other's emotional well-being as well. Asking about each other's days after a hug or a high-five can give the family time to process their emotions which can help with being able to grieve in a healthy way. I know with some parishioners, a handshake can trigger a river of tears, but in the end, they feel better because someone may have not had the opportunity to cry with someone since the loss of their child. So, checking in with one another and allowing someone to "see-in-to-me" can bring many benefits both individually and to family life. As the saying goes, "Happy-wife, happy life" and that "happy life" can enliven the family since the wife/mom is usually the heart of the family.

The physical and emotional well-being will lead to a heightened ability to connect intellectually. You may be motivated to take up a new hobby or learn a new language,

---

[43] Ibid.

something to help occupy your mind while your body heals. If you work to recover from depression or numbness, then you can start to connect on the level of reason rather than drowning in the powerful emotions that come along with losing someone you love. So intellectually, take time to connect by growing in knowledge about something together. Our minds are made to learn, so if we can learn together, families can form stronger bonds. In fact, during times of trial; the bonds need to be stronger than ever so take the time to find new things to learn about and do together.

Next, we must look at restoring confidence in a family's abilities, interest in their future, and helping them to have a desire to live their new reality. In this we must look at how each member of the family handles grief: from the dad/husband, then the children/siblings, and then the mom/wife. I leave the mom for last because biologically she is the one that has the most attachment to the little one and so will have the most to explore. We must note that in each perspective, grief is different for everyone, but more importantly, it is not something "simply to get over." There is an anonymous proverb which states this in a powerful way:

> Grief never ends...but it changes. It's a passage, not a place to stay. Grief is not a sign of weakness, nor a lack of faith...It is the price of love!

So let us look at the value of love from each family member's perspective.

Father:

In talking with men, oftentimes their reactions are hidden for assorted reasons. Some dads feel they need to be strong for their families, so they do not want to "make the space to grieve." Others are just so confused they don't know what to do. Many feel they have no place to go and so they stuff it down…sweep it under the rug. As a deacon, many men have told me the only place they have felt they could even mention it is in the confessional. This is why some men stay angry or get depressed when their wives experience a miscarriage. It must be noted, that many of the men would emphasize, they are not mad at their wives, but at the way things are. Some have gotten mad at God but were able to work through it. Many husbands have told me they don't know how to express anger in a way which does not make their wives feel uncomfortable or feel like they are getting more put on their plates. So, they withdraw and isolate. Here are some things I hear often:

> "I feel bad that I don't feel bad. I feel bad for my wife but I didn't have the opportunity to bond with the baby yet. It's her body and she did. I'm sad that she is sad."

Here's another

> "I'm supposed to be spiritual head of the family, protector, and provider. And I had no control over this. Yet I've failed in every way the head of house could" …this is why the dads take over the funeral part…it's the one thing they can do.

Doctor Perspective

Deacon Anthony makes an excellent point with regards to the difficulty men may have with expressing their emotions. Many fathers I have worked with share similar concerns when discussing how to process the loss of a child. Most want to focus on the "tactical" concerns: their wife's health, the burial of the child, and how to help any other children so their routines are not disrupted. However, once that checklist is done, they describe feeling "lost" in how to help their wives. Some also share they feel an enormous guilt because after a while they get "caught up in work, life, etc." and are not as supportive as they should be to their wife's seemingly more significant or longer lasting grief.

One father in particular, Jeff, felt comfortable describing his experience with child loss. Already a father to a 2-year-old son, he and his wife were excited about welcoming a second child when they suffered a first trimester loss at 12 weeks:

"*It didn't make sense. I knew people had miscarriages but our first pregnancy was textbook. There weren't any signs or risk factors. We went to a regular checkup. I remember being annoyed that we had to wait so long because I had a meeting after the checkup. I never expected to hear the doctor say he couldn't find a heartbeat. I told him to check again. My wife was sobbing, but I was certain he made a mistake because it was a busy day at the office and the doctor was rushing. I kept telling him to check again. He sent us to get a special ultrasound to confirm, and I was confident they would find a heartbeat, but they didn't. My wife was in shock and inconsolable. She just kept saying, we have to bury the baby, we need to call a priest. We didn't have anywhere to turn, no one seemed to know what to do with a baby that little. We finally found A Mom's Peace which helped us navigate all the red tape at the hospital who initially didn't want to release the remains of a baby under 20 weeks. They just wanted to "dispose of the tissue." I remember absolutely and probably inappropriately losing it on the medical staff. I remember cursing and yelling about them using that phrase to describe our child. I wasn't ready to accept the loss. Also, I felt like if I didn't focus on the logistics, I would have to accept the loss. I was on a mission. I had to get the remains and then find a priest, and then find a cemetery. It was my only focus. I tried to comfort my wife, but I didn't know what to say. I just tried to hold her hand. She was in physical and emotional pain and there were no words. I think as men we are not usually wired or taught to respond well to emotionally charged situations. My advice to fathers, and this may not be the right thing, but it's all I have, is ask your wife what she needs. If she knows great, if not, tell her what you do know. That you will get through this together, that you will never forget the baby, and that you will walk through the grief together as long as it takes.*

Learn from my mistakes. I think I was pretty good for the first year and then for me, life took over. For my wife, the pain and the loss really continued. I don't think I was there for her as much as I should have been. I was afraid that if I brought up the loss, it would cause her pain. What she explained later was that not a minute went by for her when she forgot the loss, and that it actually brought her comfort to talk about the baby. In our case it was twins but you know what I mean. If I had one piece of advice to give to dads, it's this: check in with your wife about how she is feeling or what she needs often. Don't get too busy that you forget that it is different for the moms because the baby lived inside them and they had a special connection. Talking about it, even if it is painful, is important."

As a psychologist when working with couples who have suffered child loss, I have found it helpful to have the couple create a list of things that are comforting and helpful. While it may sound simple, agreeing together to commemorate certain dates (i.e., what would have been the birth of the child or the anniversary of the baby's death), creating an object that memorializes the baby like a special Christmas ornament, and having a coffee date once a week to check in with each other emotionally is very helpful. Sometimes the mother wants to talk about what she is feeling and sometimes the father wants to help but does not know how, but working together to create ways to honor the baby may be mutually comforting.

Deacon Note: Isolation is one of the ways that we can lose ourselves because there is no support or accompaniment. It is the worst place to be. As men, we know this, which is why we love team activities. We relieve our stress through things such as team sports, "guy-humor" (which involves a lot of goofiness and sometimes "expensive" laughing because it may be at the "expense" of another person, but charitably and in good humor), and even competitive activities. Isolation goes against the very grain of being a man because we feel the urge to guard and support our families as well as we tend to reduce stress through *communitive* activities. The issue is we must prudently find ways to acknowledge the tension and our need to relieve stress while simultaneously not feeling as if we are going to upset our family or burden the women we love (wife, sister, etc.) with extra stress if we try to address our own grief and loss. I suggest that as a man, you can and should find peace and grieve along with your wife/sister/daughter. Here are three suggestions.

First, do not isolate yourself. Find other men who you can talk to about this situation. This "talking" may involve something active as sometimes men open up more during sports, competition, music, and/or even video games, i.e., something active. As noted earlier, isolation can, and often does, lead to desolation. So, let us stay away from desolation by staying connected to other men who can hold you up.

The second suggestion is to be brave by opening up to your family. As men, we often feel we must be strong for our families. Sometimes, however, being strong means being "man" enough to show that you can be vulnerable. To open up your heart so your family can walk through the journey of child-loss as a family and not as three, four, five, etc. (depending on how many other family members are involved) separate individuals. After all, the word for man in Latin is "vir" and "vir" is the start of virtue. *Virtue is found in the middle which means it is not a suppression of feeling/emotions/reality (one extreme) nor is it being completely non-functional and caught up in emotion (other extreme).* As men, we can lead our families but leading also means accompaniment, walking together with our families. So, men, our grief must lead to manliness, virtue. This means staying away from isolation and being virtuous in finding outlets for our grief as well as walking with our family in their grief as well.

The third suggestion is to know that as St. Paul says, "when I am weak, then I am strong" (2Cor. 12:10) or "there is power in weakness" (2Cor. 12:9). Men often feel like they are to be the protectors of their family. Since they could not protect their families from the tragedy of miscarriage, they may feel like failures. This is where ironically, the woman-who can also feel emotionally drained, must support her husband as well. It is a partnership and that means that in these times of pain you go back to the root of your marriage which is the faithful friendships which become "sturdy shelters and life-saving remedies" (Sir. 6:14, 16). As a father, you will need to, as the second suggestion notes, to open up to your family, especially your wife. It also means that you have to do things so that you can feel you are not a failure in protecting your family but can still help them to thrive. Some fathers have told me that they rediscovered old hobbies, getting back in shape, joining groups like the Knights of Columbus or Legion of Mary so they can serve their communities, or helping their other children with activities. One father I knew even helped his wife organize a fun-run to help raise awareness for those who have had miscarriages to help with funeral costs. Another father did construction and fixed up other people's nurseries so their children could have something special to live in once their baby was born. A third father started an open gym group to play basketball and then have some quick snacks to check in with each other and see how their families were doing in coping with the miscarriage. The possibilities are endless! For men, in order to get back power, you may need to do SOMETHING! Yes, you must open up and talk, but for the most part, men prefer to be active. So, finding activities that can help you to cope and process your emotions can be an important aspect in moving forward after miscarriage as a father.

The father must also find ways to initiate (even re-initiate) connections with the wife or mother of the baby that was lost (sister, friend, etc.). As noted family therapist Clayton Barbeau explains that a father must have a positive influence on the family. He writes, "[T]he father must be a positive influence in the home who must put forth positive efforts to educate those who belong to him. Wax is not molded merely by protecting it from melting; it must be worked upon with a conscious design."[44] The man must not simply focus on fixing the problem, i.e., "protecting the wax from melting"; but also, positively work upon the relationship with a conscious design which is love and sacrifice. Men must remember that sacrifice is equated with our manhood and fatherhood. Again, Barbeau notes:

> At the time of our wedding, we dedicated ourselves to giving our lives for the good of the one we love. Our heroic moments occur day in and day out-whenever we

---

[44] Clayton C. Barbeau. *The Father of the Family: A Christian Perspective* (Manchester, NH: Sophia Press Institute, 2013), p. 80.

have to deny ourselves for others. The lifelong sacrifice of ourselves to the good of others is what constitutes our fatherhood [manhood] in its fullness…How often lately have we taken back the gift of ourselves that we offered before God on our wedding day? If we have allowed "business" and the world to make us forget it, we have called back the sacrifice; we have recanted at the stake. What was meant to be our martyrdom and our triumph has become our treason and our defeat.[45]

We must remember as men, to get the power back in our manhood, we must look for the good of the ones we love, i.e., sacrifice, but also not forget about ourselves. As the Great Commandment of our Lord says, "Love your neighbor as yourself" (Matt. 22: 37-39); not instead of yourself.

Thus, as men we must cultivate the virtue of fortitude with a particular emphasis on patience so we can lead our families to cultivate this aspect of fortitude in the same way. Fortitude "perfects our capacity to do battle with that which would keep us from the good."[46] As men, we may have to do battle with our emotions, the potential to isolate ourselves or

---

[45] Clayton C. Barbeau. *The Father of the Family: A Christian Perspective* (Manchester, NH: Sophia Press Institute, 2013), p. 34.

[46] Kevin Vost. *Unearthing Your Ten Talents: A Thomistic Guide to Spiritual Growth* (Manchester, NH: Sophia Press Institute, 2009), p.74.

get angry at the situation, and even the urge to think we are powerless and failures. This is the reason we need to pray for and develop the virtues of fortitude and in a particular way, patience. Patience, "as a part of fortitude…describes our ability to endure suffering without becoming sorrowful or defeated." [47] It is quite easy as men who are experiencing a miscarriage in their families to either avoid the difficult situation due to feeling overwhelmed which is called being impatient or they become resigned to bear the hardship but give into sadness and sorrow feeling they are trapped in this sadness. Patience is the virtue to be brave and strong to endure our pain without feeling that we are trapped in hopelessness, but that we can continue to take even just one step forward in love. We must aim to take this one step as men, for the good of ourselves and our beloved families.

Children

Deacon Note:

Speaking of families, next we will look at the perspective of children who have lost a sibling. A child must deal with three big concepts. First, the child has to deal with the fact

---

[47] Kevin Vost. *Unearthing Your Ten Talents: A Thomistic Guide to Spiritual Growth* (Manchester, NH: Sophia Press Institute, 2009), p.89.

that "death" is something new to them. They may not have known anyone who died before the miscarriage. Second, we should look at affirming their human dignity so they can understand why someone is taking the time to honor human dignity. Thirdly, we need to help the child to understand how to cope with this experience in a healthy way which generally is the realm of psychology, but since grace builds on nature, God does have something to say about this issue.

First, we have to explain to children the concept of death. I have done many funerals and kids' reactions to death can range from tranquil to sobbing to completely unaware or completely consumed. I had one child put a stuffed animal at his sister's grave. Another time, a little five-year-old boy stayed behind, said a prayer and placed his favorite toy race car at his brothers' (we had to bury two of his siblings) graves with a heartfelt tear in his eye. Compare that to a funeral I was at in which the boys were playing "kill the dragon" under the pews or another funeral in which four of the kids were playing tag while we were gathering the family in front of the body. Some kids are aware of what is going on while others are not. Some kids are so aware they even think of their parents. I remember one child sat and hugged his mother for five minutes trying to comfort her to make sure she was okay since the dad did not want to attend. Another time, a young girl made flowers for her deceased sister as well as for her mom. She wanted everyone to know that her sister and mom were still all princesses and that death didn't take away their crowns. A final example was a young Latino boy about eight years old who watched his mom crying in agony while we buried her baby, his baby brother. He translated some of my comments and reflections into Spanish for the family. Twenty minutes pass with everyone in his entire family weeping bitterly except himself, he calmly walked over to me, looked upwards and said three words that touched my heart to this day. He said, "Thank you sir." Kids can be amazing!!!

This is the reason it is important to start with helping them to understand death. Some children think of death as someone hiding from us or playing "the sleeping game" (which as someone who babysits and works with kids, is one of my favorite games, especially after lunch time). These can be good analogies to help the child understand (but there can be precautions that parents need to be aware of concerning connecting death and sleep as Doctor Heisman will note later) the concept of death, but depending on their age, the simplest definition which I find most effective is death is: "the end of your earthly life." This is important to tie into the fact that we are made up of both body and soul. We have a life here on earth, as well as a life after this earth in which we choose to be with God or choose not to be with Him. The life of the deceased baby is a life in which the baby has gone to be with the God who loves him/her and loves us. It is important to emphasize that since God is love and is able to be with all of us, He does not have to choose to have either us or the baby. He has both and will continue to have both as long as we keep meeting Him in loving conversations and meetings which we call prayer. Since the baby is in the heart of God, if we can go to that heart too, we will always be united. We remember this in St. Paul words to the Romans that we mentioned previously (see Rom. 8:35-39).

We don't know how long our life is on this earth, but we do know that God has a plan for it. So, I like to use a little acronym to help kids understand death. Death:

> **D** elivers
>
> **E** veryone
>
> **A** lbeit in a mysterious way
>
> **T** o
>
> **H** im who made and loves us.

It is crucial to emphasize that the death of the baby is not a punishment for something they as siblings did (as some think their disobedience is the reason their sibling died), but is ultimately God calling their brother or sister back to Himself. I explain "mysterious way" because sometimes, often, we don't understand why God decided to take the baby when He did. We do know however that He did it in love and eventually He will call everyone back to Himself.

This brings us to the second theological point which is explaining the reason it is important to take the time to honor their deceased baby brother or sister. This gets to a fundamental question about "How do you determine the value of something in order to judge if it is worth your time?" A pastor from Ireland[48] shows generally we give four criteria to determine the worth of something.

1. How it is designed
2. Its designer
3. Its durability
4. Its demand or how rare it is

Something's worth can depend on how it is designed. If something looks good or brings joy to you when you get it, you think of it as valuable. For kids, if they get a toy they've wanted or something that could keep their attention for hours, you both would say it is valuable. Well, the little brother or sister who you are taking time to honor has been made in the "image and likeness of God" (Gen. 1:26). So, from the very fact that the little brother or sister who has died is made to be like God and to reflect Him; He is worth honoring. He or she is something breathtakingly beautiful as Scripture says, "I praise you, because I am wonderfully made" (Ps. 139:14).

---

[48] Pastor Craig Ledbetter. How Valuable is a Soul: Commentary on Mark 8:37. February 14, 2010. Accessed at: https://www.biblebc.com/Studies/OpenDoor/worth_of_a_soul.html

Next, the designer of the object makes it valuable. This is why name brands are more valuable than generic brands. For example, *Frosted Flakes* are more valuable than *Special Store Corn Flakes*. A Gucci purse is worth more than the Lucci street brand knockoff. Nike Air Jordan 19 shoes are more valuable than the Air Cruise Walmart version. It is because the person who makes the shoes gives it value. God made us and with a purpose. We are NOT accidents or there by chance. We even see that humanity is the crown of all creation as mankind was the last thing made in creation. As Psalm 138:8 states, "The Lord will fulfill his purpose for me" and again in Proverbs 19:21, "The human mind may devise many plans, but it is the purpose of the Lord that will be established."

Thirdly, how long something lasts makes it valuable. In talking with children, you could ask them what is better, a game you can play once and then you can't play anymore or a game you can play over and over again; which is better? Or in speaking to teenagers, which car is more valuable, one that will last a couple of months or one that will last for a few years? Our Lord speaks of this criterion with the parable of the person who builds his house on rock instead of sand because the house on rock lasts longer in storms (see Matt. 7:24-27). In all of these examples, we see that the one that lasts longer is more valuable. Well, our bodies may last for a time, but our souls last for all eternity because they "return back to the God who gave it" (Ecc. 12:7). Our bodies will one day be reunited with our souls which means we as persons will last for all eternity. This is the reason St. Paul writes:

> For this perishable body must put on imperishability, and this mortal body must put on immortality. When this perishable body puts on imperishability, and this mortal body puts on immortality, then the saying that is written will be fulfilled:
> "Death has been swallowed up in victory."
> "Where, O death, is your victory? Where, O death, is your sting?" (1Cor. 15:53-55).

Since all persons are immortal and will last for all eternity in the victory of Jesus who conquered death, our littlest brothers and sisters are valuable.

Fourth, something's value depends on its rarity. A common trading card is not as valuable as a trading card in which only 20 were made. A diamond is worth more than gravel or rocks because rocks are everywhere, but diamonds are not. The amazing thing is that our littlest brother or sister who has passed away is unique, one of a kind and thus is irreplaceable. This is a huge reason for taking the time to honor him or her once they have passed as well as the reason we honor all those who die.

So, we can show the child it is important to honor their deceased brother or sister because they are of the highest value based on the criteria of worth. He or she was designed in a beautiful way even in their short lives as an image of God. He or she was designed by the best and most important designer of all, God. He or she is immortal and thus will exist forever as well being a one-of-a-kind blessing. In short, they have the highest value and so should have the highest honor which is the gift of our time given to them in love. Time is the best gift because once you give it to someone you cannot get it back. Thus, we give our time to their younger brother or sister in death to give them the honor he or she deserves because they have value beyond measure. This is the reason it is a work of mercy/charity to bury the dead and to pray for them as it upholds the priceless worth of each human person; an irreplaceable gift worthy of honor and the gift of our time. Or in short, we take the time to honor their little brother or sister because a baby is a person and as we hear in the famous book Horton Hears a Who, "A person's a person no matter how small." The baby may be small, but beyond measure in his or her value and worth!

In this, we can also point out to the child that we hold every person in high esteem including the child who is asking about death. We can connect their deceased brother or sister's death and dignity to their own dignity and worth.

This brings us to the third theological point which is we need to help the child to understand how to cope with this experience in a healthy way. In general, a child may be mad or sad. It is important to let the child know that these are emotions and emotions are part of being human so they can and should be expressed. We just have to teach them how to express them in healthy ways. As noted child author Michaelene Mundy writes:

> Anger is like fire. Fire is good when it keeps us warm and helps us to cook food. But fire can sometimes get out of control. Anger can be good when it makes you want to do something about a tough situation. It can give you energy to work harder to solve a problem...Anger can help you to tell someone what's bothering you, so you can work together to work things out.[49]

Anger can be an emotion that can help give you the energy to reach out to others when you are going through a tough time in life to ask for help. It is important to let the child know that anger is a fire, but we must choose what we do with that fire. This is important because it lets the child know three crucial things about anger. First, it is an emotion and does not need to be suppressed, but does need to be directed. Second, we should not blame others or the situation for making us angry, we must take responsibility for and control our anger. Again, Mundy notes, "It's natural to want to blame someone else for making you angry. But YOU are the one who's angry, and YOU are the one who can do

---

[49] Michaelene Mundy. *Mad Isn't Bad: A Child's Book about Anger* (St. Meinrad, IN: Abbey Press, 1999).

something about it."[50] Third, we must teach children healthy ways to direct that anger and not allow it to get out of control or separate them from those who love them such as God, parents, family, and friends. This can be something as counting to five and then choosing five things to do to help others. It could be going to take some time away from the situation and then coming back once he or she is calm. Ways to direct this anger are dealt with in a big way in the field of psychology, but it is important from a theological perspective that emotions are not meant to be snuffed out, but are data points to help move us to action or to do something.

We must also mention that being sad is also natural after the death of a sibling. Mrs. Mundy notes, "When someone you care about dies, it's very sad. There will be tears, but tears can be good. Sad isn't bad."[51] Kids often think that being sad is something that they should avoid or they will possibly get punished. This is because many people indirectly teach kids that being sad is a bad thing. It is bad in the sense that it does not feel good, but like anger, it is an emotion that swells within us so that it can move us to action. We are not meant to dwell in sadness as that leads to depression, but it is a data point which you must help your child to choose what he or she wants to do with it. One way we can help a child deal

---

[50] Ibid.

[51] Michaelene Mundy. *Sad Isn't Bad: A Good-Grief Guidebook for Kids Dealing With Loss* (St. Meinrad, IN: Abbey Press, 1998).

with sadness is to help them to realize that their sadness is a natural reaction that represents their relationship to their deceased brother or sister, as part of their family bond. In order to direct that emotion, you can help them to do something to remember their deceased brother or sister such as drawing a picture or composing a song/poem about him or her. The important thing is for them to do something positive with this data point that will help build up their humanity and love their deceased brother or sister AND themselves following the Great Commandment of love of God, neighbor [in this case the deceased brother/sister], and self (Matt. 22:37-39).

I will conclude this section on children with a warm memory of going to a cemetery with a mom who lost two children through miscarriage. She told me that she takes her two surviving children to the graves on the anniversaries of their deaths and has a picnic with them. Then they all make a gift for their deceased brother and sister and say a prayer for them. She told me the kids enjoy this because it reminds them of their "bigger family" and the power of love. Love is powerful and if we can teach our children this tremendous lesson, their lives, and ours as adults too, will be all the better for it!

Doctor Perspective

From the perspective of a clinical psychologist who works primarily with children, discussing death can be complicated but important. The extent of the discussion largely depends on the age of the child. When my twins died, my son was almost 3. He knew we were expecting and was excited about having a sibling. It was a difficult conversation to have as a psychologist and a mother, to balance my feelings and what was developmentally appropriate. In our case, as he was so young, it was actually easier to explain that the baby had to go back to Heaven (that's my personal opinion, but I will offer some other options as well). My son had many questions. And we tried to answer each one patiently. In essence, we let him know that the baby was no longer in my tummy but was with God and happy there waiting for one day when we would all be together. I would caution you not to tell little ones that the deceased loved one is sleeping. While this may sound comforting initially, sometimes this leads to trouble sleeping for the kids as they start worrying about going to sleep at night and not waking up. Stick to a simple version of the truth: "Our loved one's body stopped working, and we won't be able to see them anymore." Make sure to let them know that you are sad, and that you might be sad for a while. Consider telling them about what is going to happen and what it will look like: the funeral, things that may change at the house, etc.

For older kids, it's more complicated., It is appropriate to educate them about what happens medically sometimes during a miscarriage, not in depth but that sometimes a pregnancy does not end in a birth. Miscarriage is something that happens commonly and it's okay that we grieve the loss. The most common question is "Where does the baby go?" This very much depends on your specific religious, cultural, or general belief system but the goal is to make the child not feel afraid of death, to normalize it as a natural, albeit sad, part of life. If your personal belief system allows for it, help the child understand what happened but also that the baby's soul is safe and happy in heaven or whatever is appropriate to your family. The key to the conversation is giving them an explanation that makes sense that is comforting, not scary. As a psychologist, I urge you to decide as a family what you want to share with your other children as far as what happened and how to grieve together.

It can be overwhelming to talk to children about death but I tend to follow these steps:

DO: *Tell them the truth right away.*

DO: *Give them time and space to process what's happening. They may not have questions right away but they may later. Check in with them daily to make sure they don't have anything they need to ask or that they are worried about.*

DO: *Use the actual word "death" or "dead." Do not say, "they passed away," "they are sleeping," or they "have to go away for a while." Kids have wonderful imaginations. If you try to use these phrases the kids may have questions like "passed where?" "If I go to sleep, will I never wake up? or "If they went away for a while, when are they coming back?"*

DO: *Give your child a job if there is a funeral or burial. Kids love to be helpers. They can help make a flower arrangement for the funeral, pick an object or toy to leave at the cemetery, or pick a song to be played at the burial; this helps them feel a sense of control over the loss. They may also write a letter or draw a picture.*

DONT: *Hide your feelings. Cry in front of your children, normalize that processing pain is healthy.*

DON'T: *Be angry at unexpected reactions. Kids, especially the little ones, may actually express relief that they won't be getting a new brother or sister. They don't mean it! I promise. Some kids may have been upset about getting a new sibling (because it meant they would have to share mommy and daddy and their toys) which is actually quite common. They may say something which hurts your feelings but remember it's coming from a place of innocence. If this does happen, very patiently and gently explain it hurts your feelings when they* *say this because you were excited about the baby, and even though they won't be here like we thought, they are still part of the family.*

DON'T: *Be afraid to bring up your baby. However, one word of advice. Try to make sure it's balanced. I have seen mothers who become all consumed with grief and don't get the therapeutic help they need and so become maladaptively perseverative about their loss, to the detriment of their living children. Mourn, and grieve, and talk about your beautiful children but balance the concept of death for your children. Death is not only about loss but about the possibility of new life.*

Mother

Doctor Perspective

As a mother, it's a bit more complicated. In the agony of losing a child, you are in shock and visibly upset. When your child/children ask you what's wrong, it's important to have an answer, even if it's just "Honey, Mommy's not feeling well, but I'll be okay. Can you just give me a little space to relax?" One of the most difficult things as a mother who has experienced the loss of a child is to continue to have to function whether it's in taking care of living children you may have, or having to go to work, or attend family functions. For you, the entire world stopped but for everyone else it kept going. It's also difficult when miscarriage is not as acknowledged as it should be by our society. People expect you to resume your daily routine because "it was early," or "you have other kids," or "you can try again." It should not be as difficult for people to understand that your entire world stopped when their heart did. So, when tasked with having to care for other children, or go back to work, etc., address your pain, address your needs, and set your boundaries firmly.

Grief can be all consuming. You feel as though there is a hole in you that nothing can fill. It feels so noticeable that sometimes you are surprised other people don't see it. Others describe it as drowning over and over again, waking up every day to the same torture. It does feel like that! BUT, the grief does soften, it does become tolerable, it changes. Hold on mama! Hold on! One of the best things I ever did was offer to moderate a support group for mothers and fathers who have lost a child to miscarriage or stillbirth. I, as the psychologist, was supposed to help the mothers but so many times it was bidirectional because it was so comforting to realize I wasn't losing my mind. Others were grieving and mourning just like I was, and I was not alone! The first few days you feel numb, like a zombie, not really alive but not dead. Then a few weeks go by and the exhaustion and depressive symptoms may find you. Then just when you think things are getting better, BAM, here come the panic attacks and anxiety symptoms. BUT, you are not alone! If you feel like your family, your husband, your friends, or your coworkers don't understand or are not being compassionate in ways that are helpful, then reach out to a mental health professional, reach out to support groups, reach out to other mothers who have suffered child loss. I promise you are not crazy! I promise you are not alone! And I promise you will one day be able to taste the sweet along with the bitter.

Prescription 6

Relationships with Others
(Society and Friends/Community Support)

"Let us not grow tired of doing good, for in due time we shall reap our harvest, if we do not give up. So then, while we have the opportunity, let us do good to all, but especially to those who belong to the family of the faith" (Galatians 6:9-10).

Doctor Perspective

There's an old saying that sometimes your family is not the one you are born into but the one you create (through friends and community relationships). Unfortunately, sometimes your extended or immediate family may not be a healthy source of support. So, it is critical to find that support elsewhere. While your friends may not understand what you are going through, they can help. Reach out and tell them you need help. You might not know what you need, but tell them you just want them to come over and keep you company. It will flow naturally. A mother who lost her baby at 18 weeks and whose husband was deployed at the time of her loss remembers not feeling she could turn to her family for support due to unhealthy family dynamics, so she turned to a group of friends:

> "I remember texting them and saying that I didn't know what I needed but that I could use some company." They created a shift schedule so I never had to be alone for a few weeks until my husband came home. It was incredible. They didn't try to force me to talk if I wasn't ready. They brought over books and board games and we just cooked and sat and cried and laughed. I don't know what I would have done without them. I was nervous at first to reach out and ask for help. But I'm so glad I did."

Leaning on friends during a time of loss can be extremely healthy and productive. If you are blessed enough to have some close friends, then reach out when you are ready and ask for whatever you need. Your friends will be grateful you asked.

Deacon Note:

This next prescription is necessary because families have to support one another as an individual unit and basis of society, but also society must be there to support the smaller family units. These are the Catholic Social Principles of Subsidiarity (working at the smallest level, that of the individual family, for the good of society) and Solidarity (letting everyone know we are all in this together). Community has an immensely powerful role in the healing of the family.

I know one family of six who lost their littlest brother after a medically complicated pregnancy. One of the sons was a student of mine in high school. The entire school prayed for his baby brother and mother daily even making it part of our morning prayers. We did this for months and so the little one became like an honorary little brother to everyone in my classroom. Sadly, the little one did not make it and my student was devastated. But the entire class showed up for the little one's funeral rites and it brought such comfort to the family. That family was so touched by the community support that they sent their future children to the school as well; the student in my classroom even asked me to be the deacon at his wedding. I was honored! The thing that we must realize is that when we are there for people in the bad times, they know they are loved and will be there to share good times with us. It matters that the community is there for them because everyone wants to belong to a group where they are loved during the hard times in life; they are loved even when they have a load they need help carrying; they are loved even when it's not convenient or easy. This is true friendship and love and is the foundation of community.

This is the reason the *Catechism of the Catholic Church* emphatically states, "The family must be helped and defended by appropriate social measures. Where families cannot fulfill their responsibilities, other social bodies have the duty of helping them and of supporting the institution of the family" (*CCC*, 2209). There is a duty to help and support families because there is a duty, especially in the Church Community, but also in society to live out love in an authentic Christ-like way. This means looking for ways to serve, but not in a mechanical, heartless "I've completed a task" type of way, but with heart, patience, and sincerity. This is the standard for Christians and for all humanity because of our dignity in being made in the image and likeness of God. So, Jesus tells us, "Whatever you did for the least of my brothers and sisters, you did for me" (Matt. 25:40). Hopefully, we would not mechanically do something for someone we truly love and who truly loves us. We must as a society and Church community look to walk with others and help them take heart during their time of miscarriage/stillbirth grief.

Pope Saint John Paul II tells us this when he wrote, "The role of those who care for depressed persons and who do not have a specifically therapeutic task consists above all in helping them to ***rediscover their self-esteem, confidence in their own abilities, interest in the future, the desire to live***. It is therefore important to stretch out a hand to the sick, to make them perceive the tenderness of God, to integrate them into a community of faith and life in which they can feel accepted, understood, supported, respected; in a word, in which they can love and be loved [emphasis mine]."[52]

We have seen this quotation from Pope John Paul II before, but now we can apply it to the family. First, let us look at groups that can help families rediscover their self-esteem as John Paul calls it, but which we will refer to as their sense of hope and control over their journey. This is primarily support groups where members of the family can feel that they are not alone, are not people who "messed up," as one father put it, "with their reproductive abilities," (to be clear, this is not true, but this is often descriptive of the guilt couples sometimes feel after dealing with miscarriage and infertility) and to help them discover and use the tools they have to walk towards healing. The community can form groups connecting people with similar experiences; this can bring tremendous healing. We have a bereavement group at my parish, and it has helped many people continue on their journey of life after the loss of loved ones. This could be revolutionary because miscarriage and stillbirths are still taboo topics in society. I've given homilies on it, and often I have lines of

---

[52] Pope John Paul II. *Address of John Paul II: To the Participants in the 18th International Conference Promoted by the Pontifical Council for Health Pastoral Care on the Theme of "Depression"*, sec. 3. Friday, 14 November, 2003. Accessed at: https://www.vatican.va/content/john-paul-ii/en/speeches/2003/november/documents/hf_jp-ii_spe_20031114_pc-hlthwork.html

women and families thanking me for addressing the topic. I've posted some of these homilies, and I've had people from across the country thank me for, as one woman told me, for finally helping her to see she "had the permission to talk about it as a Christian." It is sad that many families think this is something they must keep to themselves because it is "not proper Church-talk." The Church and other communities forming groups to walk with moms and families during this time of grief shows that this is a significant issue and God and the Church care about their family's miscarriage/stillbirth. This also helps them to know they are not alone and have others that are going through the same situation. Another often overlooked issue is marital problems following the loss of a child. Marital issues that often arise after a miscarriage or stillbirth can be difficult to discuss with clergy. Having an opportunity to discuss these concerns with other couples would be hugely beneficial.

Another beneficial group would be a group that springs into action immediately following the miscarriage or stillbirth. These can be groups that help families plan a burial or memorial service for their babies upholding their dignity and worth. Regarding funeral services, sometimes family and friends are willing to assist with funeral arrangements. It's nice to have help but be cautious here as well. I have seen parents receive too much help and then look back and see "the one big thing" they could have done for their child was done by someone else and they were full of regret. There are many things to consider and perhaps assigning help is better. Can you pick up the flowers? Can you pick up the prayer cards? Will you help me write a program? Giving away these tasks are a personal choice. There are many choices to be made. Will there be an in- ground burial or will the baby be cremated? Will the hospital release the baby to us or do we need to contact a reputable funeral home? It's worth asking the hospital about the release of the baby's remains if it's something you'd be interested in doing. It is your legal and religious right to care for your miscarried baby's remains. Hospital policies and state laws will regulate how you do that, but it can be done. Know your rights. That's why another great group would be a group that can provide pro-bono legal services for when parents need help with legal questions regarding their child's remains.

A third group of people can help cook food for the family while they heal and take care of things like funeral services or medical appointments. Another example would be a group who can provide financial assistance to help offset the cost of a burial. Funerals can be expensive and an often-unexpected cost (sometimes costing thousands of dollars).

There also can be a group of clergy who train other clergy in dealing with miscarriage or bringing awareness about it during their formation. This will help clergy be aware of how common these experiences are in their parish, to know and understand the tools the Church has given them to help them shepherd their flock during those times of grief, as well as help them to understand the point of view of the families who are coming to them for help or whom they need to seek out because they think there is nothing in the Church to help them. There is a huge gap that needs to be filled for groups that can be formed to help bring comfort and tangible help to families experiencing child loss. One in four babies are miscarried or stillborn, so we, as a community, should make sure there are organizations and plans in place to walk with those who are going through this time of grief.

A fifth group that would be helpful is a group to provide solidarity to help the family continue to feel supported and remain connected to the community, and to help the family keep the memory of their deceased baby alive. These could be prayer groups that come and pray with the families during the anniversary of their child's death, so they know that their bigger Church family has not forgotten them or their littlest brother or sister of the community. This can be a group of people who have had a miscarriage or stillbirth and get together for lunch just to help each other have "normalcy" in life and to grow as friends. It can be groups that knit or create things to honor the deceased babies to give to the families at the burial service.

Most of all, there need to be groups that can help couples, maybe an anonymous group of people that advertise a help line at their local parish or the community that can simply give couples information about what to do when they are having a miscarriage or stillbirth. Most couples and/or individuals have no idea what to do themselves or for their baby when they experience a miscarriage or stillbirth because it is hardly ever talked about in society. This group or parish help line would be a critical added support system that needs to exist! These types of groups exist but there are not enough at the moment. These groups can help each family or parent who has experienced a miscarriage to know they are not alone. This reminds me of an old Chinese Parable in which we will end this prescription for community:

An old emperor had many sons, who were often looking out for themselves. When the father had exerted his authority, and tried to get them to work together but to no avail, he called them together, looked around in the forest, and wisely used another means of teaching them a lesson. He ordered his sons to be called before him and a short bundle of sticks to be brought in. Then he commanded them, one by one, to try to break the bundle. He told them if they could, they would get all their inheritance. So, they tried, but to no avail. The sticks being closely and compactly bound up together, it was impossible for them to break it. After this, the father ordered the bundle to be untied, and gave a single stick to each of his sons, at the same time bidding each son to break it. Each did so with great ease. The father then addressed his sons:

"O my sons, behold the power of unity! For, if you in like manner, would but keep yourselves strictly conjoined in the bonds of friendship and love, there is nothing that can break you; but when once the ties of brotherly affection and love are dissolved, how soon do you fall to pieces."

God does not want us to fall to pieces. He calls us as a community to stay united through all tragedies, including miscarriage. Let us aim to be like the bundle of sticks, a firm support for our sisters and brothers who have lost a child, so they can be united to the bond of unbreakable love; thus, not easily broken. This is the power of unity! We must always remember "unity" is what completes "community." Let us always aim to help one another be made whole.

Prescription 7

Engagement in Healing (Conclusion)

"It is not the will of your heavenly Father that one of these little ones be lost" (Matthew 18:14).

Doctor Perspective

It has been a privilege to contribute to this guide for families who have experienced child loss through miscarriage and stillbirth. There is so much more that could be included in this book, but our hope is to provide a simple guide to help families in a time of crisis. As a psychologist, I urge you to make your mental health a priority after suffering such a great tragedy. Please seek therapeutic help. This is not something that should be done alone. You are not alone!

It has been an honor to work with Deacon Anthony (even though we don't always agree) because despite having widely differing views on many things, religion and science and respect can coexist!

This poem by Mary Frye has always brought a sense of comfort so I would like to share it with you:

> Do not stand at my grave and weep,
> I am not there, I do not sleep.

I am a thousand winds that blow.

I am the diamond glint on snow.

I am the sunlight on ripened grain.

I am the gentle autumn rain.

When you wake in the morning hush,

I am the swift, uplifting rush

Of quiet birds in circling flight.

I am the soft starlight at night.

Do not stand at my grave and weep.

I am not there, I do not sleep.

Do not stand at my grave and cry.

I am not there, I did not die!

As a mother, I say to you, on those nights when the world has gone to sleep and you are kept awake by the hole in your heart and soul, please know that there are thousands of mothers grieving with you. You did not fail as a mother, you succeeded. You gave your beautiful little one a safe and loving home for as long as humanly possible. When you are alone and those burning tears fall from your cheeks, know that you are the best mother in the world because you would have and still would give your life to have been able to save your child; that is the love of a mother. And you are a mother! You are the bravest mother to wake up every morning and continue to fight, to fight for yourself, your family, ALL of your children…to live and thrive even when exhausted, even when you feel alone and without hope! Your baby chose you to be its mother, whether in this life or the next. So, remember, the next time you feel you can't breathe because of the ache in your heart, the next time everything around you is drowned out by the sobs emanating from your soul, the next time you feel like you cannot get out of bed...we see you. We love you! You are a mother to a child you cannot hold but you are a mother to a child you will always love and who loves you too!

Deacon's note:

In the beginning of this book, we told you that we as a doctor and deacon would give you some prescriptions to help breathe again and A.C.Q.U.I.R.E peace. Breathing is critical for life and existence, both naturally and supernaturally and so we have given you Seven Prescriptions to breathe again. It is interesting because the Hebrew word *Ruah* has both a natural and supernatural meaning as it means breath, wind, and/or spirit. Naturally, breath is the air needed to fill our lungs so we can function. Wind is a source of power to help things to move and grow such as in sailing or windmills for electricity. Supernaturally, the Holy Spirit is the breath of God which gives us life as a new creation and connects to Love who is God. We hope our prescriptions help you to breathe, soar and move to new dimensions in life, and be filled with the Spirit so you are inspired to take in the breath of God, hold His hand, and walk together towards the peace He has made you to have.

That peace is a journey which involves many parts, a lining on top of the grains of sand as we spoke of in the oyster analogy at the beginning of the book. These linings are the various parts of our humanity which need healing and when united can obtain the pearl of great price, the beautiful Oyster of having peace in life, even after the tragedy of miscarriage. We have prescriptions to help you with each step of the way. First, we give tips on Attaining prudence and knowledge explaining things we should and should not do to help people going through a miscarriage. Then we spoke of advice to Care for your mind and to gain a healthy psychological perspective. Third, we gave lots of information about the medical perspective with Questions about the body's response to miscarriage/stillbirth, especially the medical condition of microchimerism which physically connects us to our deceased loved ones. Fourth, we gained spiritual keys by Unlocking God's perspective in miscarriage helping people to see how to look at miscarriage from a perspective of wisdom and encourage those in the Church to do more to be icons of God's love communicating a position of accompaniment rather than abandonment. Fifth, we looked at the Intersecting perspectives of the family members, examining how the father, children, and mother are grieving in different ways, but love has the last word in each type of grieving. Sixth, we examined the Relationships with groups outside of the family and how they can support families going through miscarriage or stillbirth. Finally, we encourage an Engagement in healing so that everyone can know their worth and know they are not alone when this happens since it occurs in one of four pregnancies.

Breathing and being able to ACQUIRE peace is the goal of this book. This book is not an exhaustive be all and end all on the topic of miscarriages and stillbirths. We hope it makes a positive contribution to the topic, but more importantly that it contributes to helping the reader, whether you are someone who has experienced a miscarriage, a friend who is trying to support someone who has had a miscarriage, or even someone who is looking to be an advocate to help find resources and break the taboo of the topic.

I especially hope, as deacon, to inspire more clergy to get involved with the everyday tasks of helping people to be aware of miscarriage in wedding preparations and homilies so there is not a shock if it occurs in their marriages, in walking and comforting families through giving them resources in their Church communities and being a visible sign of Christ's love to those families who have had a miscarriage/stillbirth. I pray we can help families to open up about this cross which needs to be infused with the reassuring breath of God's goodness and love.

In the end, we must make the choice to breathe again, to accept the inspirations of God's help to take even just one small step on the journey from grief to grace. This means being bold enough not to ask for a cure, but to embrace the healing process. The cure is just to fix the problem, to focus simply on the thing that is wrong so it doesn't hurt us anymore. God wants to heal us, that is to make us whole both body and soul *despite* the problem, so that we can have peace which only He can give. We must remember that Jesus did not cure everyone. He **cured some** like the woman who was hemorrhaging and touched his cloak (Matt. 9:18-22), a leper (Matt. 8:1-4), and the demonic (Mk. 5:1-20); but He wants to **heal all**. In God's mysterious plan, He chooses to **miraculously cure some people** of their ailments (we may not be *cured* from the mental anguish of having a miscarriage). However, even if we are not cured, we **still have hope because He wants to make everyone whole**. Thus, some of the last words Jesus tells us in Scripture is, "Behold, I make **all things new**" (Rev.21:5) [emphasis mine].

To be made new, we must repeat the words of the Centurion, "Lord, I am not worthy that you should enter under my roof, but only say the word and my servant **shall be healed**" (Matt. 8:8) [emphasis mine]. We may not be cured from the trauma of miscarriage, but God can make us whole despite it; in that we are healed. We must be bold and "say the word"; follow the prescriptions and take the next step towards healing. This healing, being made whole, may take a lifetime (remember we are not pretending to offer a guaranteed "cure" for miscarriage; that would be beyond our paygrade as a deacon and doctor), but it is still worth the journey. As a mother and author whose family struggles with depression as well as someone who has training in counseling, Jeannie Ewing writes:

> Let us climb the mountain of Love singing, knowing that pain or joy, everything that happens to us, can only increase the love of Jesus in our hearts and the peace which surpasses all understanding...Grief is the catalyst that ignites the spark of zeal in our hearts and sets ablaze that yearning, that pining to love God wholeheartedly instead of halfheartedly. When we suffer, God adds firewood to the flame in our hearts, which both refines...and extinguishes all that is not of Him. When the fire smolders into embers, He picks up the ashes and creates an entirely new masterpiece of our lives.

The Lord wants to make a new masterpiece out of our lives, to heal us instead of simply curing us from miscarriage. Remember the transformation process from Chapter 2. Healing does not mean you will never have sorrow. The secret is turning all pain and sorrow to sacrifice by uniting it to divine love. In this, we learn to breathe again and turn sorrow and pain into something beautiful.

Danielle Erwin, a mother who has gone through the grief of miscarriage expresses this beautifully in her poem entitled *Beauty from Pain*:

Write it out

Share your doubt

Hesitate a minute

Is your heart truly in it

Do you really believe

Others will see what you perceive

Will they look past the words

And understand your hurt

That this is your way

Pain leaves through words you say

You're trying to make your return

Prayin' you're not spurned

Your try and cleave

Praying they don't leave

They're your sanity this moment

Comfort as you lament

Tears fall and land below

On the seed ready to grow

Let it out and give it room

For from your heart, beauty blooms

It is from the heart which beauty blooms. The question is what do we keep in our hearts while being on the cross of miscarriage? Do we keep *pain* in our hearts and thus allow this situation to steal our joy, peace, and serenity? Or do we choose to be like the oyster who turns *sacrifice* into a beautiful pearl?

In this, we allow *beauty to bloom* and healing to take place. We know that there is a cross in miscarriage, but we pray that through these prescriptions, the beauty of God's blessings flourish in your life; that peace, the ability to breathe again, keeping the connection to your baby while meeting him/her in the merciful heart of Christ, and having the courage to "say the word and be healed" (Matt. 8:8). Fill these prescriptions often, especially when it is hard, and in doing so, remember happiness is filled with layers of bitterness/sand, but also grace-filled linings which ultimately will lead to the Pearl of Great Price which you can treasure in your heart.

It has been my great honor writing these prescriptions for you with Dr. Heisman and so we sign off with our prescription pad which summarizes these prescriptions. It shows theology and psychology "hearing one another" like a stethoscope by being united in God's Sacred Heart, our Good Shephard present with His baby lambs who are the miscarried or stillborn little ones , and the means to ACQUIRE trust in our loving and Merciful God who will guide you along the way. We wish to leave you with a prescription for navigating child loss, but also with hope for your journey along the way!

Appendices

Appendix I

Resources

Here is a list of resources to help in your journey. This list is not by any means exhaustive, but we hope it can help in some small way to know that you are not alone and there are resources out there to help during this time of grief. Please feel free to use these as recommendations as well.

Here is a list of resources to help in your journey. This list is not by any means exhaustive, but we hope it can help in some small way to know that you are not alone and there are resources to help. Please feel free to use these as recommendations as well.

Support

1. A Mom's Peace
   P.O. Box 534
   Nokesville, VA 20182
   571-781-2419
   Website: www.amomspeace.org

2. Red Bird Ministries (A Catholic grief support group for those who have lost a child from pregnancy through adulthood)
333 Waterford Place
Breaux Bridge, LA 70517
Website: www.redbird.love

3. Heaven's Gain Ministries
6962 Harrison Avenue
Cincinnati, OH 45247
513-607-6083
Website: https://heavensgain.org/

4. M.E.N.D (Mommies Enduring Neonatal Death)
P.O. BOX 631566
Irving, TX 75063
972-506-9000
Website: https://www.mend.org

5. Miscarriage Matters, Inc. & Miscarriage Matters 2 Men (Men's support group)
420 Spotsylvania Mall Drive #41242
Fredericksburg, VA 22407
Email: miscarriagem@mymiscarriagematters.org
833-MM-HELPS (833-664-3577)
Websites: https://www.mymiscarriagematters.org and

https://www.mymiscarriagematters.org/miscarriage-mattes-2-men

6. Footprints Ministry
   6605 Mallard Park Drive
   Charlotte, NC 28269
   704-509-6603
   Website: https://www.angelfire.com/ny5/footprints-ministry/index.html

7. Hannah's Prayer/Hannah's Tears
   Website: https://hannahstears.org

8. Comfort Zone Camp
   6606 West Broad Street
   Suite 401
   Richmond, VA 23230
    804-377-3430
    Website: www.comfortzonecamp.org

9. A Memory Grows
   P.O. Box 34282
   Fort Worth, TX 76162
   682-214-4608
   Website: https://amemorygrows.org/home

10. Caleb Ministries
    608 Matthews-Mint Hill Road, Suite 109
    Matthews, NC 28105
    704-841-1320
    Website: https://www.calebministries.org/

11. Haven Network
    124 North Water Street, Suite 201
    Rockford, IL 61107
    815-962-1512
    Website: https://www.thehavennetwork.org

12. H.A.N.D. (Helping Hand After Neonatal Death)
    P.O. Box 341
    Los Gatos, CA 95031
    888-908-4263
    Website: http://handonline.org/en/home

13. Indiana Cuddle Cot Campaign
    P.O. Box 2293
    Richmond, IN 47375
    937-733-9252
    Website: https://www.indianacuddlecotcam-
    paign.com

14. M.I.S.S. (Mothers In Sympathy & Support)
   P.O. Box 9195
   Austin, TX
   602-279-6477 or 1-888-455-6477
   Website: https://www.missfoundation.org

15. Project Sweet Pea
   45 Boylston Street
   Warwick, RI 02889
   Website: https://www.projectsweetpeas.com

16. National Share (pregnancy and infant loss support)
   402 Jackson Street
   St. Charles, MO 63301
   800-821-6819
   Website: https://nationalshare.org

17. UNITE, Inc.
   P.O. Box 298
   Oxford, PA 19363
   484-758-0002
   Website: http://unitegriefsupport.org

18. International Vasa Previa Foundation
   P.O. Box 215
   Chester, IL 62233
   267-790-6693

Website: https://vasaprevia.com

19. Empty Cradle
    31938 Temecula Pkwy, Ste A #385
    Temecula, CA 92592
    (619) 573-6515
    Website: https://emptycradle.org

20. Grief Watch
    14511 NE 10TH AVE, STE E
    VANCOUVER, WA 98685
    360-433-2527
    Website: https:griefwatch.com/

Support during delivery

1. Birthwaves (doulas who help with delivery during a miscarriage or stillbirth)
   800-518-1758
   Website: http://birthwaves.org/about-us/

2. Indiana Cuddle Cot Campaign
   P.O. Box 2293
   Richmond, IN 47375
   937-733-9252
   Website: https://www.indianacuddlecotcampaign.com

3. Project Sweet Pea
   45 Boylston Street
   Warwick, RI 02889
   Website: https://www.projectsweetpeas.com

Support for Multiple Child Loss

1. A Mom's Peace
   P.O. Box 534
   Nokesville, VA 20182
   571-781-2419
   Website: www.amomspeace.org

2. CLIMB (Center for Loss In Multiple Birth)
   P.O. Box 190401
   Anchorage, AK 99519
   Website: https://www.climb-support.org

Keepsakes & Remembrance Gifts

1. Heaven's Gain Ministries
   6962 Harrison Avenue
   Cincinnati, OH 45247
   513-607-6083
   Website: https://heavensgain.org/

2. M.E.N.D (Mommies Enduring Neonatal Death)
   P.O. Box 631566
   Irving, TX 75063
   972-506-9000
   Website: https://www.mend.org

3. Indiana Cuddle Cot Campaign
   P.O. Box 2293
   Richmond, IN 47375
   937-733-9252
   Website: https://www.indianacuddlecotcampaign.com

4. Project Sweet Pea
   45 Boylston Street
   Warwick, RI 02889
   Website: https://www.projectsweetpeas.com

5. Remembering Our Babies
   1324 Porta Rose Lane
   League City, TX 77573
   Website: https://www.october15th.com

6. Grief Watch
   14511 NE 10th Ave, Suite E
   Vancouver, WA 98685
   360-433-2527
   Website: https:griefwatch.com/

Marriage Support

    1. Footprints Ministry
       6605 Mallard Park Drive
       Charlotte, NC 28269
       704-509-6603
       Website: https://www.angelfire.com/ny5/footprints-ministry/index.html

    2. HAND (Helping Hand After Neonatal Death)
       P.O. Box 341
       Los Gatos, CA 95031
       888-908-4263
       Website: http://handonline.org/en/home

Sibling Support

    1. Comfort Zone Camp
       6606 West Broad Street, Suite 401
       Richmond, VA 23230
       804-377-3430
       Website: www.comfortzonecamp.org

    2. HAND (Helping Hand After Neonatal Death)
       P.O. Box 341
       Los Gatos, CA 95031
       888-908-4263

Website: http://handonline.org/en/home

Financial Support for Burials

1. Angel Names Association
   P.O. Box 423
   Saratoga Springs, NY 12866
   518-654-2411
   Website: http://angelnames.org

Prayer and Information

1. A Mom's Peace
   P.O. Box 534
   Nokesville, VA 20182
   571-781-2419
   Website: www.amomspeace.org

2. Hannah's Tears
   Website: https://hannahstears.org

3. ACD (Alveolar Capillary Dysplasia) Association
   12115 Henderson Hill Road
   Huntsville, NC 28078
   Website: https://acdassociation.org

4. A Memory Grows
   P.O. Box 34282
   Fort Worth, TX 76162
   682-214-4608
   Website: https://amemorygrows.org/home

5. Haven Network
   124 North Water Street, Suite 201
   Rockford, IL 61107
   815-962-1512
   Website: https://www.thehavennetwork.org

6. Indiana Cuddle Cot Campaign
   P.O. Box 2293
   Richmond, IN 47375
   937-733-9252
   Website: https://www.indianacuddlecotcam-paign.com

7. IRIS (Infants Remembered In Silence)
   218 Third Avenue, NW
   Fairbault, MN 55021
   507-334-4748
   Website: https://irisremembers.com

8. MISS (Mothers In Sympathy & Support)
   P.O. Box 9195
   Austin, TX
   602-279-6477 or 1-888-455-6477
   Website: https://www.missfoundation.org

9. NEC Society
   140 B Street, Suite 5, #128
   Davis, CA 95616
   Website: https://necsociety.org

10. Remembering Our Babies
    1324 Porta Rose Lane
    League City, TX 77573
    Website: https://www.october15th.com

11. National Share (pregnancy and infant Loss)
    402 Jackson Street
    St. Charles, MO 63301
    800-821-6819
    Website: https://nationalshare.org

13. UNITE, Inc.
    P.O. Box 298
    Oxford, PA 19363
    484-758-0002
    Website: http://unitegriefsupport.org

Books we can recommend

Miscarriage and the Saints

Everts, Cassie and Patrick O'Hearn. *Nursery of Heaven: Miscarriage, Stillbirth, and Infant Loss in the Lives of the Saints and Today's Parents.* Contemplative Heart Press, 2019.

Miscarriage, Sacraments and Grief

Breaux, Kelly. *Hiding in the Upper Room: How the Catholic Sacraments Healed Me From the Grief of Child Loss-A Memoir.* Louisiana: Kelly Breaux, 2020.

Edminsten, Karen. *After Miscarriage: A Catholic Woman's Companion to Healing and Hope.* Servant Books, 2012.

Appendix II

Medical Definitions

The Centers for Disease Control and Prevention (CDC) defines:

Pregnancy loss: Spontaneous pregnancy demise.

>**Early pregnancy loss:** Spontaneous pregnancy demise before 10 weeks of gestational age (before 8th developmental week.)

>**Non-visualized pregnancy loss:** Spontaneous pregnancy demise based on decreasing serum or urinary β-hCG levels and non-localization on ultrasound.

>**Biochemical pregnancy loss:** Spontaneous pregnancy demise prior to five weeks of pregnancy based on decreasing hCG levels, without an ultrasound evaluation.

There are also other types of pregnancies that may result in miscarriage

Ectopic pregnancy: Ultrasonic or surgical visualization of a pregnancy outside of the uterus, usually in a fallopian tube.

Blighted ovum (anembryonic pregnancy): A blighted ovum happens when cells stop growing very early in the pregnancy. Instead of developing further, the embryo is reabsorbed, causing a miscarriage. The pregnancy sac, where the baby should have grown, sometimes continues to develop.

Molar pregnancy: a pregnancy that fails to develop properly from conception. It can be either complete or partial and usually the child's remains need to be surgically removed.

Miscarriage: The unintentional pregnancy loss of a child that is under 20 weeks old; an intrauterine pregnancy demise confirmed by ultrasound or histology.

Early miscarriage: Intrauterine pregnancy loss 12 weeks or less on ultrasound.

Anembryonic (empty sac) miscarriage: Intrauterine pregnancy loss with a gestational sac but without a yolk sac or an embryo on ultrasound .

Yolk sac miscarriage: Intrauterine pregnancy loss with a gestational sac and yolk sac, without an embryo on ultrasound.

Embryonic miscarriage: Intrauterine pregnancy loss with an embryo lacking cardiac activity on ultrasound.

Fetal miscarriage: Pregnancy loss 10 weeks or greater ultrasound.

Missed miscarriage (also known as a delayed or a silent miscarriage) the baby had died but stayed inside the uterus.

Incomplete miscarriage: An incomplete miscarriage is when a miscarriage begins, but the pregnancy doesn't release from the womb.

Recurrent miscarriage: Doctors define this as three or more miscarriages in a row.

Late miscarriage: Refers to a miscarriage that happens between 14 and 24 weeks of pregnancy.

Threatened miscarriage: Signs of a possible miscarriage are called a "threatened miscarriage." Some bleeding or pain intermittent or continuous lasting days or weeks. Can continue to have a healthy pregnancy or end in a miscarriage. Rarely anything medically can be done.

Complete miscarriage: All of the pregnancy tissue has left the uterus.

Stillbirth: The unintentional pregnancy loss of a child that is 20 weeks or older.

Early stillbirth is a fetal death occurring between 20 and 27 completed weeks of pregnancy.
Late stillbirth occurs between 28 and 36 completed pregnancy weeks.

A **Term** stillbirth occurs between 37 or more completed pregnancy weeks.[53]

Term stillbirth occurs between 37 or more completed pregnancy weeks.

---

[53] Center For Disease Control. *Stillbirth*. Accessed at: https://www.cdc.gov/ncbddd/stillbirth/facts.html

Medical Terminology[54]

Anembryonic gestation: This involves a positive pregnancy in the uterus without an embryo, often referred to as a blighted ovum.

Incomplete Abortion: This occurs when not all the pregnancy tissue has passed out of your uterus

Missed Abortion: Your baby has stopped developing and your uterus has not begun the process of ejecting the pregnancy tissue. It is often not accompanied by bleeding or cramping.

Spontaneous Abortion: This is what you will likely see in your medical records. This means your body has passed all the tissue associated with a pregnancy without any medical intervention like medication or a D&C procedure. However, it has become general practice to refer to any miscarriage as a spontaneous abortion, even those that do require intervention.

---

[54] White, Kate, M.D. *Your Guide to Miscarriage and Pregnancy Loss-Hope and Healing When You're No Longer Expecting It.* Rochester, MN: Mayo Clinic Press, 2021.

Fetal Growth & Development

Fertilization: When the egg is fertilized by the sperm. Once the egg is fertilized it becomes something new called a blastocyst.[55]

Blastocyst: The term for a fertilized egg. The blastocyst will develop into two separate parts. The outer cells develop into the placenta. …the placenta carries nutrients and oxygen to and waste materials away from the fetus. **The inner cells of the blastocyst will form into the embryo.** The amniotic sac will form an inner layer of membranes that will fill with amniotic fluids, which will protect the developing embryo for the remainder of the pregnancy.

Embryo: The embryonic stage of development is characterized by the formation of the external body structures and internal *organs*. Approximately three weeks after fertilization, the embryo begins taking on a human shape. Major blood vessels form around day 17 and the heart begins to pump blood through the vessels at

---

[55] Michelle Lawson. *Healthfully.* "Child Stage Development in the Womb." 13 June, 2017. Accessed at: https://healthfully.com/81426-week-fetus-look-like.html .

around day 20. The embryo will enter the fetal stage of development at week eight of pregnancy.[56]

Fetus: Around week eight, the embryo is now called a fetus. *The lungs, brain, kidneys, and liver are beginning to function and the fetus has distinct fingerprints.* According to Discovery Health, the fetus will measure about three inches long and weigh approximately an ounce at *12 weeks gestation. During this stage of development, the external sex organs become visible on an ultrasound.* Tiny hairs called lanugo begin to cover the baby's entire body. *At approximately 40 weeks gestation, the fetus is considered full-term and ready to make the journey through the birth canal.*[57]

Note that at about 12 weeks the external sex organs become visible. If you miscarry before then, you can prayerfully consider if you are going to honor a son or daughter. There are now blood tests that you can take at 10 weeks that will let you know the sex of the baby in many cases; however, they are not always accurate. Many mothers give a male and female name for their baby if they miscarry before 12 weeks but will know their true name and honor that son or daughter by name with the

---

[56] Ibid.

[57] Ibid.

Lord and guardian angels once He reveals it. Scripture tells us, "I will never erase his name from the book of life but will acknowledge his name in the presence of my Father and of His angels" (Rev. 3:5).

If the blastocyst separates but does not become an embryo, it can lead to another condition called a blighted ovum.

Blighted Ovum: A blighted ovum, also called an anembryonic pregnancy, occurs when an early embryo never develops or stops developing, is resorbed and leaves an empty gestational sac. A blighted ovum usually occurs early in pregnancy — sometimes before you even know you're pregnant. However, you may be aware of your early pregnancy because of a positive pregnancy test or missed menstrual cycle. A pregnancy test may be positive because the early embryo secretes a pregnancy hormone — human chorionic gonadotropin (HCG) — until the embryo stops developing and fails to implant.

Helpful Miscellaneous Terms

Report of Spontaneous Fetal Demise a report submitted to the health department describing the pregnancy including factors of demise.

Combo Box, Angel Box, Cherub Box: a funeral home term used to describe a casket and vault combination to serve as an interment vessel.

Open/ Close Fee: the opening of the earth in preparation for a burial and the returning of or closing the earth into the grave.

Appendix III

Baptism of Desire

Baptism of desire (in voto): This does NOT replace the Sacrament of Baptism but can achieve some of the effects of baptism by linking a person to the body of Christ as a means of salvation. Baptism of desire IS NOT something we can do like getting baptized. Jimmy Akin explains:

> Historically, the Church has taught that the graces of baptism can be received not only through the administration of the sacrament itself (baptism of water) but also through the desire for the sacrament (baptism of desire) or through martyrdom for Christ (baptism of blood). Recent doctrinal development has made clear that it is possible for one to receive baptism of desire by an implicit desire... It is true that baptism is required for full incorporation into the Church (CCC 837), but it is not true that all of the unbaptized are unlinked in any way with the Church. This is something the Church has always been aware of.... In the thirteenth century, and in response to the question whether a man can be saved without baptism, Thomas Aquinas replied: "the sacrament of baptism may be wanting to anyone in reality but

not in desire; for instance, when a man wishes to be baptized but by some ill chance he is forestalled by death before receiving baptism. And such a man can obtain salvation without being actually baptized, on account of his desire for baptism, which desire is the outcome of faith that works by charity, whereby God, whose power is not tied to the visible sacraments, sanctifies man inwardly." (*Summa Theologia* III:68:2, cf. III:66:11–12). As these passages indicate, Catholics have historically understood that what ***is absolutely necessary for salvation is a salvific link to the body of Christ, not full incorporation into it.*** To use the terms Catholic theology has classically used, one can be a member of the Church by desire (*in voto*) rather than in reality (*in re*) [emphasis mine].[58]

This is based on the following Scriptural evidence:

- The Good thief whom the Lord promised salvation outside of water and spirit baptism due to his contrition and act of faith (Lk. 23:39-43.)
- The Holy Spirit falling upon Cornelius (symbol of sanctification and linking to Christ) before he and

---

[58] Jimmy Akin. Catholic Answers. "Baptism of Desire". Publish Feb. 1, 2000. Accessed at: https://www.catholic.com/magazine/print-edition/baptism-of-desire

those listening to Peter were formally baptized (see Acts 10: 44-48.)

- "Those who love me I also love, and those who seek me find me" (Proverbs 8:17)
- "Above all, let your love for one another be intense, because love covers a multitude of sins" (1 Pet. 4:8)

It was also supported throughout the history of the Church:

1. "I find that not only suffering for the sake of Christ can replace that which is lacking in Baptism, but also *faith and conversion of the heart*, if perhaps the shortness of the time does not permit the celebration of the mystery of baptism" (written about 400 AD.)[59]

2. Justification from original sin cannot be obtained "except through the laver [washing] of regeneration (i.e. baptism of water) or *a desire for it*" (*voto*) [emphasis mine].[60]

One last key point with this term which must be noted. An article on Baptism of desire notes:

---

[59] St. Augustine. *On Baptism*, Book IV, chapter XXII. Accessed at: https://www.newadvent.org/fathers/14084.htm

[60] Council of Trent. Session VI, Chapter IV. Promulgated January 13, 1547. Accessed at: http://www.thecounciloftrent.com/ch6.htm

The Church has always held that Baptism of water is a necessary means for salvation. However, a Baptism "in voto" can replace it when it becomes a physical or moral impossibility provided that the recipient place no obstacle nor show any contempt for the sacrament. The Fathers characterized this "baptismus fluminis" by faith, interior conversion of the heart, and a true desire to receive the sacrament: "baptizari in voluntate."*Distinction:* <u>From the part of God</u>— that He, first of all, gives the person actual graces, and then, for being docile to these divine movements, this recipient will have sanctifying grace or justifying grace infused by God upon his soul. For this Baptism "in voto," which "reconciles the person with God, delivers him from original sin and infuses supernatural life," *is essentially a supernatural act that cannot be elicited by man's natural power, nor can he dispose himself by himself for it.* <u>From the part of the recipient</u>— With the infusion of sanctifying grace on the recipient, the person under this supernatural influence makes an act of his free will, an act of faith, and contrition [emphasis mine].[61]

---

[61] Catholic Apologetics. "Baptism of Desire and Blood". Accessed at: http://www.catholicapologetics.info/modernproblems/currenterrors/bdesire.htm .

In short, baptism of desire IS NOT something we can do like when we go and physically get baptized. **It is God applying the effects of the Sacrament of Baptism; namely salvation, cleansing of Original Sin, and being linked to Christ, to a person who would have desired to be united to Jesus Christ.** Since it is the faith of the Church supplied for the child during infant baptism (See Acts 2:38-39. An example of baptism of children found in Acts 16:15 in which the entire household including children were baptized), it would seem that the faith of the parent as a member of the Church could be supplied for the necessary faith which disposes a soul to receive the particular grace of the effects of baptism known as a baptism of desire.

Some other terms of note are pastoral terms which can help someone to understand what is involved with the eternal destiny of the little ones who are lost as well as for the burial service itself.

Baptism: The ordinary Sacramental means which introduces the divine life into a person. It is mandated by Christ who said, "Amen, amen, I say to you, no one can enter the kingdom of God without being born of water and Spirit" (Jn. 3:5).

Baptism of blood & Martyrdom: This does NOT replace the Sacrament but achieves the effects of baptism by incorporating a person into the love of God by following God's promptings to have the greatest love, to "lay down his life for a friend" (Jn. 15:13) and that friend is God. Catholic Culture continues the definition: "Martyrdom in the case of a person who died for the Christian faith before he or she could receive the sacrament. The effects of martyrdom and baptism by blood are the complete remission of sin and the title to immediate entrance into heaven. The expression entered the Christian vocabulary during the first three centuries when many catechumens awaiting baptism and pagans suddenly converted to the Christian faith were martyred before they could receive formal baptism of water."[62]

Baptism of desire (in voto): This does NOT replace the Sacrament either but can achieve some of the effects of baptism by linking a person to the body of Christ as a means of salvation. Baptism of desire IS NOT something we can do like when we physically go and get baptized. **It is God applying the effects of the Sacrament of Baptism; namely salvation, cleansing of original sin, and being linked to Christ, to a person who would have desired to be united to Jesus Christ (See Appendix III for a fuller explanation).**

---

[62] Catholic Culture. "Baptism of Blood". Accessed at: https://www.catholicculture.org/culture/library/dictionary/index.cfm?id=32084

Appendix IV

Ask the Deacon

Understanding the Dignity of the Human Person
Pertaining to the Internment of Babies

Clergy and others may wrongly believe there are some babies lost in miscarriage that are too young to bury, like those who died only a couple of weeks into the pregnancy. It is critical to understand that regardless of gestational age, every single human that exists is deserving of a proper interment because every human being is made in the image and likeness of God (Gen. 1:26). No number of weeks, days, minutes or even seconds that a human exists can change the fact that each of us is deserving. Our dignity is rooted in that scriptural fact and what follows is that clergy can be confident of offering funeral rites to every single miscarried baby from the moment of its conception. As Fr. Tad says, a zygote or embryo "is not a potential human being, but a human being with potential." Hence, our last appendix will have the actual rites that can be used for the burial of a miscarried or stillborn child.

Appendix V

Rites of Christian Burial & Blessing of Parents

Since the faith of the Church community, particularly the parents and godparents, that are necessary for the Sacrament of Baptism (see *Catechism of the Catholic Church* sec. 1253-1255)[1], the consent of at least one of the afore mentioned is necessary for Christian Funeral Rites.

If that consent is given, the Child can thus have an ecclesiastical funeral (Can. 1183.2) offered on his/her behalf for an unbaptized child in the Order of Christian Funerals since the parents desired their child to be Christian just as catechumens can receive Christian burial even if they die before they come into the Church (See *Order of Christian Funerals*#18/Canon 1183.2 in Code of Canon Law):

"The celebration of the Christian funeral brings hope and consolation to the living. While proclaiming the Gospel of Jesus Christ and witnessing to Christian hope in the resurrection, the funeral rites also recall to all who take part in them God's mercy and judgment and meet the human need to turn always to God in times of crisis...*The Church calls each member of Christ's Body* — priest, deacon, layperson — *to participate in the*

ministry of consolation: to care for the dying, to pray for
the dead, to comfort those who mourn" (*Order of Chris-*
tian Funerals#7-8) [emphasis mine].

Therefore, I give an overall outline of the Rites that can be administered for a miscarried or stillborn child.

****

[1] CCC#1253-1255: Baptism is the sacrament of faith. But faith needs the community of believers. It is only within the faith of the Church that each of the faithful can believe. The faith required for Baptism is not a perfect and mature faith, but a beginning that is called to develop. The catechumen or the godparent is asked: "What do you ask of God's Church?" The response is: "Faith!" For all the baptized, children or adults, faith must grow after Baptism... Preparation for Baptism leads only to the threshold of new life. Baptism is the source of that new life in Christ from which the entire Christian life springs forth. For the grace of Baptism to unfold, the parents' help is important. So too is the role of the godfather and godmother, who must be firm believers, able and ready to help the newly baptized - child or adult on the road of Christian life. Their task is a truly ecclesial function (officium). The whole ecclesial community bears some responsibility for the development and safeguarding of the grace given at Baptism (emphasis mine).

Ceremony Overview

3 Parts to Ceremony

- Blessing of grieving parents (from the *Book of Blessings #279-294*)
- Transfer of the body to place of committal (*Order of Christian Funerals*#121-126)
- Rite of Committal with Final Commendation of Infant (*Order of Christian Funerals*#327-336/337-342)

Overview

1. **Blessing of parents** (from the Book of Blessings #279-294)

   § Start by blessing the parents to bring them comfort and to know the Church is embracing them as they bury their miscarried or stillborn son/daughter

   § (Optional): Naming of Child

   A. To be done immediately after the Preparation prayer (#285 Book of Blessings)

   § Scripture Readings (or see Book of Blessings #287 for other options of readings)

B. Reading: Lam. 3:17-18, 21-26, 33 or Rom. 8:31-38

§ Homily by Deacon/Priest
§ "Prayer of Blessing" from Rite of Parents after a Miscarriage

2. **Transfer of the Body to Place of Committal** (Order of Christian Funerals, #121-126)

§ Invitation
§ Scripture Verse
§ Litany of Mercy/Solace (Order of Christian Funerals#123)
§ Concluding Prayer
§ Invitation to the Procession

3. **Rite of Committal with Final Commendation** (Order of Christian Funerals, #327-336)

§ Invitation to Committal
§ Scripture Verse
§ Prayer over Place of Committal (includes blessing of gravesite)
§ Invitation to Prayer (Option C for a child who died before baptism)
§ Silence

§ Prayer of Commendation (Option B for a child who died before baptism)

§ Committal (place casket into the grave)

- Burial and placing of flowers

§ Prayer Over the People and Final Blessing

Bibliography

Akin, Jimmy. Catholic Answers. (2000, February 1). "Baptism of Desire". https://www.catholic.com/magazine/print-edition/baptism-of-desire.

American Psychiatric Association. Diagnostic and statistical manual of mental disorders (5th ed.). Washington DC: American Psychiatric Association, 2013.

Anthony, Gerard-Marie. Who Am I: The Theology of the Body in Prayer. Waterford, MI: Bezalel Books, 2011.

Apologetics, Catholic. (n.d). Baptism of Desire and Blood. http://www.catholicapologetics.info/modernproblems/currenterrors/bdesire.htm.

Aquinas. Summa Theologica. https://www.newadvent.org/summa/1016.htm.

Augustine, Saint. On Baptism: Against the Donatist, Book IV. https://www.newadvent.org/fathers/14084.htm

Barbeau, Clayton C. The Father of the Family: A Christian Perspective. Manchester, NH: Sophia Press Institute, 2013.

Bishops, United States Conference of Catholic. National Directory of the Formation, Ministry, and Life of the Permanent Diaconate. Washington DC: USCCB Publishing, 2005.

Cameron, Fr. Peter John. The Noonday Devil: Acedia. Catholic Education Resource Center. https://www.catholic-education.org/en/religion-and-philosophy/spiritual-life/acedia-30-06-17.html

Canon Law Society of America. Code of Canon Law: Latin-English Edition, New English Translation. Washington, DC: Canon Law Society of America, 1983.

Catholic Book Publishing Corporation. Book of Blessings. New York, NY: Catholic Book Publishing Corporation, 1989.

Catholic Book Publishing Corporation. Order of Christian Funerals Including Appendix 2: Cremation. New York, NY: Catholic Book Publishing Corporation, 1998.

Centers for Disease Control and Prevention. What is Stillbirth? (2020, November 16). Centers for Disease Control and Prevention. https://www.cdc.gov/ncbddd/stillbirth/facts.html.

Collazo, Julie. U.S. Catholic. (2016, November). The quiet grief of miscarriage: The Church Needs a Better Pastoral Response Toward Women and Families Who Experience Miscarriage and Stillbirth. http://www.uscatholic.org/articles/201610/quiet-grief-miscarriage-30794 .

Culture, Catholic. (n.d). Baptism of Blood. https://www.catholicculture.org/culture/library/dictionary/index.cfm?id=32084.

Erwin, Danielle. Holding On: Poems on Coping with Loss After Miscarriage. Middletown, DE: Danielle Erwin, 2019.

Foundation, Robert Wood Johnson. Miscarriage or Stillbirth Increases Risk of Breakup or Divorce. Accessed at: https://www.rwjf.org/en/library/articles-and-news/2010/11/miscarriage-or-stillbirth-increases-risk-of-breakup-or-divorce.html

Hudgins, James Hudgins. St. John of the Cross, Fathers of the Church Lecture Series Part III. All Saints Catholic Church, CD, 2005.

Hunter-Kilmar, Meg. Aleteia. (2020, May 16). Saints Who Battled Mental Illness. https://aleteia.org/2020/05/16/saints-who-battled-mental-illness.

John Paul II, Pope. (2003, November 14). Address of John Paul II: To the Participants in the 18th International Conference Promoted by the Pontifical Council for Health Pastoral Care on the Theme of "Depression." https://www.vatican.va/content/john-paul-ii/en/speeches/2003/november/documents/hf_jp-ii_spe_20031114_pc-hlthwork.html.

Jones, Jonathan. Greater Good Magazine. (2018, November 16). Why Physical Touch Matters for Your Well-Being: Physical contact seems to be declining in modern life. But what happens when we lack human touch? https://greatergood.berkeley.edu/article/item/why_physical_touch_matters_for_your_well_being.

Kamper-Jorgenssen, Mads et al., (2014, February) "Male Microchimerism and Survival among Women," International Journal of Epidemiology 43.1. http://doi.org/10. 1093/ije/dyt230.

Kheriaty, Aaron and Fr. John Cihak. The Catholic Guide to Depression: How the Saints, the Sacraments, and Psychiatry Can Help You Break Its Grip and Find Happiness Again. Sophia Institute Press: Manchester, New Hampshire, 2012.

Lawson, Michelle. Healthfully. (2017, June 13). "Child Stage Development in the Womb." https://healthfully.com/ 81426-week-fetus-look-like.html.

Ledbetter, Craig. (2010, February 14). How Valuable is a Soul: Commentary on Mark 8:37. https://www.biblebc.com/Studies/OpenDoor/worth_of_a_soul.html.

LeJuene, Marcel. Catholic Missionary Disciples. (n.d). Catholic Parenting - How To Do Everything You Can To Get Your Kid To Heaven! https://catholicmissionarydisciples.com/news/catholic-parenting .

Libreria Editrice Vaticana. Catechism of the Catholic Church. United States Catholic Conference Inc.-Libreria Editrice Vaticana, (Trans.; 2nd ed), Citta del Vaticano: Libreria Editrice Vaticana, 1997.

Mayo Clinic. (2021, September 21). Blighted Ovum: What Causes It? https://www.mayoclinic.org/diseases-conditions/pregnancy-loss-miscarriage/expert-answers/blighted-ovum/faq-20057783.

_____. (2021, October 19). Dilation and curettage (D&C). https://www.mayoclinic.org/tests-procedures/ dilation-and-curettage/about/pac-20384910.

_____. (2020, May 13). Labor Induction. https:// www.mayoclinic.org/tests-procedures/labor-induc- tion/about/pac-20385141.

_____. (2021, October 16). Miscarriage. https://www. mayoclinic.org/diseases-conditions/pregnancy-loss- miscarriage/symptoms-causes/syc-20354298.

Miller, Ricky. (n.d). Social Intimacy. https://rickeymillerpsy- chologist.com/research .

Miravalle, John-Mark L. Beauty: What it Is & Why It Mat- ters. Manchester, New Hampshire: Sophia Press, 2019.

Miscarriage Support, Catholic. (n.d). Quotes on Suffering. https://www.catholicmiscarriagesupport.com/emo- tional/quotes-on-suffering/.

Mundy, Michaelene. Mad Isn't Bad: A Child's Book about Anger. St. Meinrad, IN: Abbey Press, 1999.

_____. Sad Isn't Bad: A Good-Grief Guidebook for Kids Dealing With Loss. St. Meinrad, IN: Abbey Press, 1998.

New American Bible, Revised Edition. Washington DC: Confraternity of Christian Doctrine, 2010.

Pace, Rachel. (n.d). 6 Forms of Intimacy to Build a Strong Marriage: Incorporate These Types of Intimacy into Your Relationship and Watch Your Marriage Thrive. https://www.beliefnet.com/love-family/relationships/

marriage/6-forms-of-intimacy-to-build-a-strong-mar-riage.aspx.

Parker, Colin Murray. Bereavement: Studies of Grief in Adult Life. Routledge, 2nd Edition, 2009.

Sheen, Fulton J. Go to Heaven: A Spiritual Roadmap to Eternity. San Francisco, CA: Ignatius Press, 2017.

_____. Life is Worth Living: San Francisco, CA: Ignatius Press, 1999.

Shott, Heather Morgan. Today Show. (2016, October 21). "I am 1 in 4': Mom's viral campaign shows just how common miscarriage is. https://www.today.com/parents/miscarriage-affects-1-4-women-see-some-their-stories-t104234

Trent, Ecumenical Council of. (1547, January 13). On Justification . http://www.thecounciloftrent.com/ch6.htm

Vatican II, Ecumenical Council of. (1965, December 7). Gaudium et Spes: Pastoral Constitution on the Church in the Modern World. https://www.vatican.va/archive/hist_councils/ii_vatican_council/documents/vat-ii_const_19651207_gaudium-et-spes_en.html.

Vost, Kevin. Unearthing Your Ten Talents: A Thomistic Guide to Spiritual Growth. Manchester, NH: Sophia Press Institute, 2009.

White, Kate. Your Guide to Miscarriage and Pregnancy Loss: Hope and Healing When You're No Longer Expecting It. Rochester, MN: Mayo Clinic Press, 2021.

Wilson, Ralph. (n.d). Moses: The Reluctant Leader- Section 4: Grumbling, Conflict, and Delegation (Exodus 15-18). http://www.jesuswalk.com/moses/4_grumbling.htm.

Wright, Viona. Consolation and Desolation. IgnatianSpirituality.com-A Service of Loyola Press. https://www.ignatianspirituality.com/consolation-and-desolation-2